THE
BOY WHO
WOULDN'T
DIE

THE
BOY WHO
WOULDN'T
DIE

DAVID NYUOL VINCENT
WITH CAROL NADER

FAIRFAX BOOKS
ALLEN&UNWIN

This edition published in 2013
First published in 2012

Fairfax Books, an imprint of
Allen & Unwin
83 Alexander Street
Crows Nest NSW 2065
Australia
Phone: (61 2) 8425 0100
Email: info@allenandunwin.com
Web: www.allenandunwin.com

Cataloguing-in-Publication details are available
from the National Library of Australia
www.trove.nla.gov.au

ISBN 978 1 74331 552 1

Set in Adobe Garamond by Post Pre-press Group, Australia
Printed and bound in Australia by Griffin Press

10 9 8 7 6 5

MIX
Paper from
responsible sources
FSC® C009448

The paper in this book is FSC® certified.
FSC® promotes environmentally responsible,
socially beneficial and economically viable
management of the world's forests.

To all the Lost Boys of South Sudan, especially those who did not survive the war. To all those who have not had the opportunity I have had to write this book. And to my mother Tereza Anthony Joko Ngomu, and my sister Abuk.

Please take a moment to remember the more than two million people who perished during the Sudanese civil war. May their souls rest in peace.

Contents

Prologue

I willed my body to be invisible as I lay flat on my stomach, face pressed into the dusty ground, waiting.

My head jerked up at the sound of a woman screaming in the distance. The plane would return any second—sent from northern Sudan to kill us. And there was this hysterical woman whose arm had been blown off in the first blast, running around, spouting blood, wailing and drawing attention to herself. I glared at the woman. Did she want them to take her other arm, too?

I knew the plane would be back. The enemy liked to play with us. They'd hover over us in the sky and drop a bomb or two or three or four and then take off, wanting us to think they were done with us. Then they'd return for another hit.

I exchanged a look with my friend Dominic, lying on the dirt nearby. Did we have enough time? We got up, ran to the woman and shoved her to the ground.

She had a sheet draped around her body. We held her down, removed the sheet and pressed it to the bloody flesh where her arm used to be. And we waited.

The arseholes were predictable. But this time, we were ready for them. Our three bodies remained pressed to the ground as it was mercilessly pummelled around us.

Just minutes ago I had been a normal kid riding a borrowed bike, all thoughts of politics and war and men determined to kill me out of my head. I had been so immersed in riding the bike that I hadn't heard the plane flying over our heads.

The first warning I had had of imminent danger was when I glanced over my shoulder and saw that Dominic was no longer standing. Another airstrike! There had been no time to dive into our makeshift trench. I had quickly jumped off the bike and thrown myself onto the ground. Man, I had been lucky.

I was so sick of this shit. I was sick of running, of being hunted.

I was thirteen years old. I knew how to pull apart a gun and re-assemble it with devastating efficiency. I had been trained to kill.

I had watched my friends die, and then buried their bodies. I had watched people literally starve to death. With every death, and the thought of my sisters and Mama being raped and killed, the anger had burned inside me until I had wanted to pick up a gun and kill. I had wanted to go to the front line of this interminable war. I had been willing to get myself killed.

But I no longer had ambitions to be a soldier. I wanted to abandon Sudan. I wanted a new life. I thought I could fight this war in a different way—I had briefly tasted the fruit of education and I wanted more.

I didn't know if Mama and my sisters were dead. I had a new cause now, and that was to live. I would be of no use to my family dead.

We were running out of places to run to in Sudan. As long as we stayed here, the men with the guns and the planes would continue to hunt us.

It was time to get out of Sudan forever.

Sudan was Africa's largest country geographically, until the south separated from the north in 2011. Prior to that, it was one nation with a politically troubled history. Its neighbours included Kenya, Ethiopia and Uganda to the south and Egypt and Libya to the north, with the River Nile running through its entire length.

The largely impoverished Sudanese people speak Arabic and many other tribal languages. They have endured decades of war. The first raged from 1955 to 1972. The battle flared again in 1983 with a second civil war—one that proved to be even more deadly.

Each war pitted the mainly Muslim Arabs of the north against the mainly Christian population in the south. The conflict's causes are many and complex: religion, power, the north eyeing off the oil resources of the south, and the south's long-held desire to be autonomous.

While South Sudan is the world's newest nation, it remains plagued by conflict—and its people continue to be at war with each other.

1

The End of Play

Bodies slick with sweat, we walked in silence. To talk was to waste energy.

I looked closely at my father's face, searching for something that would reassure me. But all I saw was fear.

Don't die, don't die, don't die, don't die. I chanted the words in my head like a mantra.

I didn't want Baba to worry about me, so I kept walking, feet hot and aching, grimacing through my pain and exhaustion. It was Baba who slumped to the ground first and closed his eyes.

I grabbed his shoulder and shook him with surprising energy for a child who was famished and parched. I was struggling to keep my own eyes open but knew I had to keep awake for both of us.

My father was a stranger to me, but I needed him. He was all that I had, since the night he had come home and grimly taken me away. That had been weeks ago, and we had been walking ever since.

As Baba's eyelids continued to droop, I shook him furiously. 'I'm awake,' he mumbled, opening his eyes briefly and then closing them again.

Please don't die, Baba, I thought, shaking him with growing urgency.

∎

The day I walked barefoot out of my life, I carried nothing. No food or water. I wasn't even wearing a T-shirt. We had to leave immediately. We had to leave in a way that didn't arouse suspicion. We had to pretend we were returning soon. Except we weren't.

Baba had come home after his latest long absence. He always went away, and I never knew where to. I spent much of my childhood wondering whether he was dead.

When he returned, he'd always pick me up and give me a lolly. Happy to be in his arms, I'd forgive him for leaving us again. But today, things had been different.

He had come to the house and I had run to greet him the way I always did. I had immediately sensed that something was wrong. He didn't pick me up this time. Grim-faced, he had gone directly to Mama and moved her away for a private conversation.

Worried, I had strained my ears. Their voices were raised but I couldn't make out their words. Mama had come back first—tears streaming down her face. I wondered what they had been fighting about. I wanted to tell her that whatever it was that had made her cry, it would be OK. She had moved towards me—she couldn't stop crying. Baba had ushered my older sister Abuk and me towards the door. Mama's tears didn't stop the whole time.

It had all happened so quickly. Now, as we stood outside the house, Baba and Abuk and me, I was frightened and confused. Baba wouldn't tell us what was going on. He told us we were going on a brief trip. Judging by Mama's tears, I guessed she and my other sisters, Katerina and Lidia, weren't coming with us.

Then, the walking started. I didn't realise it at the time, but it was a walk that would abruptly end life as I knew it. It was a walk that would mean the end of play.

■

I could tell that my friend knew he was in deep shit as he let out a long wail. And it was all because of one tattered pair of shoes.

The trouble began when he took off his shoes and thought it

would be hilarious to tie them together and toss them high over a wire, so they dangled between two electricity poles. But where we come from, even the most dilapidated shoes are precious. The boy's triumph transformed into panic as it dawned on him that he'd face his mother's fury if he went home without his shoes.

About ten of us stood beneath the shoes arguing over the most efficient way to get them and stop our friend's damned wailing. But throwing them up and over the wire had been the easy bit. Getting them down would be trickier.

The others thought there was no way one of us could climb the pole and get them. It was too high and too dangerous.

But I was a competitive and cocky little boy, and I didn't like anyone telling me what I couldn't do. I decided that I'd show the others—I'd climb the pole and retrieve the shoes. My friends scoffed at my plan, convinced that a little kid couldn't pull his skinny body up that pole. But I knew I could do it.

With the confidence of the very young and stupid, I began my climb. Ignorance makes you fearless, and I easily reached the top. The shoes were hanging not far from the pole, but still too far for me. I reached out but couldn't touch them. I tried to grab the wire so I could move closer to my goal. I was five years old. It didn't occur to me that electricity could kill.

'Stop! Don't do it!' nine boys shouted at me.

'What do you want me to do?' I asked, climbing down.

One of the boys found a stick and handed it to me. 'Knock the shoes off with the stick,' he said.

I repeated my climb and perched on the post, stretching out and using the stick to give the shoes a good whack. They flew off the wire and landed near their still-wailing owner's feet. I climbed down the post a hero. I had just initiated a very dangerous game.

I was born in Wau, in the Western Bahr el Ghazal state of southern Sudan. And I was a cheeky kid.

I hung out with other boys of varying ages. We formed a crew and found ways to entertain ourselves. Climbing the electricity poles became a favourite game after my first epic ascent. We had to play this game early in the morning or late in the day, as the blazing African sun made the metal pole hot enough to scald your skin. We'd race each other to the top. I learnt to manoeuvre my body around the pole and pull myself up with lightning speed. I always won.

My resourcefulness would later come in handy, instilling resilience in me and giving me crucial survival skills. But I didn't know it yet.

For most of my life I didn't even know my own age. We didn't celebrate birthdays in Sudan, and many of us didn't have birth certificates. It wasn't until I was a grown man that I learnt I had been five when the war began its devastating surge through southern Sudan.

For a long time, my friends and I didn't feel it. We ran around oblivious to the danger that was sweeping through our country. I was one of the youngest in our group, but I had earned the respect of the older boys with my courage.

We met each morning beneath the mango trees at the playground and plotted the activity of the day. Sometimes it was making toy cars carved out of tin sheets. I wasn't good at making them—but I was so good at stealing the tin from the factory that it became my job. I'd climb over the fence, grab as much tin as I could throw over the fence, and make a bolt for it. Workers at the factory tried to catch me but I was always too quick. Even when my limbs were entangled in the fence and I got deep cuts on my body, I wasn't deterred.

One day, while going about my tin-stealing duties, I grabbed the wire on the fence and cut myself, leaving a massive gash on the palm of my left hand. It was bleeding and stinging badly. Going home and taking my chances with Mama wasn't going to happen. Her punishment was always painfully effective—she'd grab the tiny bit of fat around my waist and twist until it hurt so much my eyes filled with tears. But I cried only at first. Later my pride took over.

One of the boys suggested I could take out the sting by peeing on my injury. I was sceptical, but I thought it was a more appealing option than facing my angry mama. So I cupped my right hand and, on cue, peed into it. I wasn't even grossed out as I rubbed the pee into my left palm.

Maybe I was so frightened of Mama that I willed this unconventional remedy to work. Or maybe its medicinal effect was all in my head. In any case, I must have thought it worked, because peeing became our medical solution to lots of things. Wau is a rocky town and—being allowed to wear shoes only on special occasions—I mostly ran around barefoot. Sometimes I'd stub my bare toe on a rock so badly that my nail would begin to peel off. My cure was to hover over my toe and pee on it. My own pee was my first-aid kit.

This was how we filled our days—running around Wau, the rotten stench of fallen mangoes filling our nostrils, daring each other to do crazy, stupid things.

We even had a competition to see who could kill the most birds. Mama's brother, my uncle Fadul, made me a rubber sling and taught me how to shoot them. All the boys kept a tally of their kills—each notch on your sling represented one dead bird.

Sometimes we brought our dead birds home to eat. Home was a hut with mud-brick walls and a grass-thatched roof. It was a traditional African hut with no telephone and no electricity, let alone a television.

The bath was outside the house in a shed surrounded by trees. I hated bath time. There was no shower or hot water. Instead, you tipped a bucket of cold water over your head. My older sisters Katerina, Lidia and Abuk, or occasionally Mama, bathed me every night until I learnt to do it myself. I would do anything to avoid the soap that made my eyes sting. So I came up with a sneaky way to pretend that I had had a bath—by dabbing water onto my body to give the appearance of being wet.

Our family was too poor for us to go to school. But despite having a naturally curious mind, I didn't miss learning. What I really longed for was a school uniform. Our more wealthy neighbours who had moved to Wau from northern Sudan dressed each day in a uniform, with a white cotton shirt, navy blue shorts, and nice shoes. They looked really smart. I wanted to be one of the kids wearing the nice uniform.

Instead, I usually spent my days wearing nothing more than a pair of shorts, shirtless and shoeless. We saved our good clothes—a pair of pants and a shirt—for Sundays, when we went to the Catholic church. It was the only time we were allowed to wear shoes. Going to church was a big deal; we socialised with other families and proudly wore our nice clothes.

We looked forward to Christmas, too. It was the only time we'd get new clothes. We went to Mass on Christmas Eve, and it was such a drag. I would have preferred to play with my friends outside. Church went on for hours and I'd sit there fidgeting in my nice clothes, not listening to the priest and wanting it to be over so we could go visiting and get sweets and cakes. It was a rare time when I felt like there was enough food.

I was used to not eating enough. On an amazing day, we got to have two meals. But one meal a day was more normal. As for breakfast, well, that was a concept that was foreign to me.

Despite food being scarce, my mama Tereza made the effort to be creative. To sweeten her tea, she would drop a lolly into her cup to make up for the sugar we couldn't afford. We had no oven, so Mama did all the cooking in pots wonkily placed on top of burning wood and charcoal. Rice and meat were rare treats. We virtually lived on sorghum, a grain commonly found in southern Sudan. We ate it with soup or vegetables, and somehow I never tired of it. Mama cooked it in different ways, with various greens. I know she worked very hard and tried her best. Poverty makes you hard and Mama was stern.

Our simple lives were in stark contrast to that of our neighbours. I was friendly with the kids and sometimes they'd invite me to come over and eat with them. This infuriated Mama, because she didn't want her children to be seen as beggars. But I couldn't help it—my goal was simply to eat.

The thing about hunger is it unfolds in stages. First, you feel that you really want to eat and you satisfy that feeling by eating. If there's no food and no way of filling your belly, the urge to eat grows. But if it lasts for hours and hours, you get to the point where the hunger is dulled and replaced by a huge emptiness. Then you move on and find ways to distract yourself. Eventually, you forget you are hungry.

I took a philosophical approach to hunger very early on; I learnt to accept that today was one of those days when I might not eat, that I would have to look for food, that I would go through the hunger stages. Usually when a hungry baby cries, it is promptly fed by its parents. But I learnt that crying wouldn't make the food come. Hunger, like poverty, hardens you. By the time I was about two years old, I was tough.

Despite the harsh conditions in which we lived, I think I was happy. My life was strangely idyllic; I didn't know what I was missing out on. Playtime was more important to me than eating. If you took playtime away from me, I would have missed it more than food. So our group filled the days hunting birds and grasshoppers, climbing the poles and the mango trees, trying not to think about how hungry we were, not wanting playtime to end. But it did.

■

I can't pinpoint the exact moment I observed that danger had entered our town. Playtime gradually became less and less. I wasn't seeing much of my friends. Some mornings we woke to stories that people had been killed while we slept, but those stories didn't make sense to me. The conflict seemed to be happening in a faraway place. Until the night we heard gunshots outside our hut and Mama pushed us to the ground. The war had landed on our doorstep.

Mama was spending more time at home, making sure we were indoors. If we played, it was within our own compound only. Mama had used to let us run around outside for half the night. Now, we had to be inside by 6 p.m. The whole street was strangely quiet by then. All you could hear was the dogs barking, the army men outside, the occasional gunshot. We didn't risk making loud sounds from inside our hut. We didn't want to draw attention to ourselves. We had heard rumours that the armed forces would beat people—usually the men of the house—and take them away. Often, we heard, those taken away didn't come back.

As the situation became more desperate, my father, Vincent Mangok Ayuel, wasn't around much. Baba came from the village Turalei, almost 200 kilometres north of Wau. His movements were mysterious to me—he never told us where he was going or where he had been. He was from the Dinka tribe, and that made him a target. It was a Dinka man who was leading the rebels—the Sudan People's Liberation Army—and the uprising against the north.

Not only was Baba a target for the north, but for other tribes in the south, too. As the war's body count piled up, some southern tribes blamed the Dinkas for inflicting the war upon all of them.

Baba was an educated man—he had attended a school run by missionaries. He could speak English, and had joined the fight during the first civil war in Sudan, before fleeing across the border to the Central African Republic. He didn't return to Sudan until the war was over, and then came to Wau. That's where he met Mama, who is from the Bai tribe, a smaller tribe in the south. That makes me a half-breed.

I pieced together these early recollections of my life many years later. I must have been eight when playtime ended. The conflict had entered Wau, the fighting had intensified, people had lost their homes and there was an exodus of refugees from a seemingly endless war. One day, Baba and Abuk and I joined them.

I didn't guess that we wouldn't come back. I concluded that we were going on a short trip, and Mama was crying because she'd miss us. But we'd see her again soon. I didn't know it at the time, but Mama was pregnant. There was no way a pregnant woman could have accompanied us on such a dangerous journey.

The second Sudanese civil war began in 1983, when the Sudan People's Liberation Army from the south—the military arm of the Sudan People's Liberation Movement—entered a fierce battle with the northern-based forces of the government of Sudan. Thousands of rebels were led by John Garang de Mabior, a Dinka man from the south who dreamed of a different Sudan.

The movement was formed after a peace agreement that had ended the first civil war—known as the Addis Ababa Agreement of 1972—was violated by Sudanese president Jaafar Nimeiri. A key part of that agreement had been to give the people of the south greater autonomy. The tension was compounded when Nimeiri, who had abolished parliament soon after seizing power, introduced Islamic Sharia law into the nation. After growing unrest, he was deposed in a coup in 1985 and Al-Jazuli Daf'allah was installed as prime minister. He resigned from the position when elections were held in 1986, and was replaced by Sadiq al-Mahdi.

The second Sudanese civil war remains one of the world's most devastating conflicts. It persisted for more than two decades, killing an estimated two million people and displacing millions of others. Many children were orphaned or separated from their parents and forced to fend for themselves as the war raged.

2

Walking to Nowhere

As my father took Abuk and me away, he couldn't have known what would happen to all of us. There was a cold logic to his decision—if a family was divided, the odds were greater that at least some of them would survive. But the likelihood of survival was reduced if an entire family stayed together. It was a gamble made by many families in southern Sudan, and one that caused so many to be separated during the war.

We left Wau while it was still daylight. The sun was at its most brutal, but we had no choice. A man and two children leaving their home in the middle of the night would have attracted attention and placed us at risk of being questioned—or worse—by the men with the guns.

We walked at a steady pace until we got to a point near a river, where there were more men with guns. They must have been friendly, because Baba had a brief conversation with them before they let us board a small boat for the short cruise across the river. Then the walking continued.

It was a tough walk for a kid, especially barefoot. Sometimes Baba picked me up and carried me for a bit, but he never answered my questions. We walked for hours that first day, cupping our hands and drinking from the streams that we passed. I tried to mimic my sister's bravery. Abuk was a couple of years older than me, but immediately assumed the role of my protector.

We walked in silence, interrupted only when Baba whispered urgently for us to hide in the bushes. When he sensed danger was near, we dived into the nearest bush. I tried to make myself as invisible as I could while we waited for the danger to pass. I unquestioningly obeyed him. My father wasn't armed. He wouldn't have been able to protect us if we bumped into hostile people—people who wouldn't have hesitated to kill us.

We reached a point where there were more men with guns. It was a rebel post, and for the first time, I got a true sense of the danger of what we were attempting. The men looked at Baba suspiciously. Maybe they thought he was a spy sent from the north. They asked him lots of questions, and then dragged him away. I stood nervously with Abuk and waited for him to come back, terrified that he wouldn't. But he was lucky—one of the men knew him. For the first time that day, we had food, and I ate hungrily. This was where we would sleep.

I'd never slept out in the open before and I really didn't relish the idea now. I couldn't decide which was more terrifying—the men with the guns or the lions, hyenas and other wild animals that were lurking in the darkness. I couldn't shake off the fear as Baba and Abuk and I lay side by side on a large sheet that Baba had found. That was our bed; a mosquito net was our doona. I stared up at the dark sky, unable to sleep, hoping we wouldn't have any more nights like this, wondering what the hell was going on.

■

The tough, hot ground blistered my bare feet as we started walking again. Baba dipped my aching feet into water whenever we stopped at a stream.

Baba talked to some fishermen that we came across and asked them for fish. We cooked it over a fire made with twigs and branches, resting beneath a tree while we ate, until Baba told us it was time to move again.

I frequently asked him where we were going, and when we would get there. His answer was always the same: 'Tomorrow we'll get there.'

Tomorrow would come and I'd ask him again. 'Tomorrow,' he'd repeat, until I grew tired of asking.

I wanted to go home, to Mama, to my friends, to play. Life before this hadn't been perfect, but I knew no better. At least then we had fun. This walking wasn't fun at all. I felt the tears come and I couldn't stop them. I didn't want to be a baby, but I couldn't help the loud sobs. 'I don't want to walk anymore, Baba,' I cried.

He looked at me. 'Keep going. We'll be there soon.'

The goodwill of village people who gave us food helped to keep us alive. But the people weren't always generous and at times we'd walk on, denied food, hoping we'd be luckier in the next village.

Abuk never cried. Sometimes she held my hand. We walked all day and sometimes well into the night. My father's walk was unwavering; he walked with a steely determination to reach his destination.

After a few days we arrived, famished and exhausted, in the village called Turalei, where my father came from. I had fantasised that when we finally reached our destination there'd be food waiting for us. Instead, we were greeted with the shocking fact that no-one spoke our language, Arabic. Baba's family spoke only their native tongue of Dinka.

It was the final straw for Abuk and me. Up until this point, we had been very brave. I had given in to tears only once; Abuk not at all. Now that we had paused our long walk, we thought hard about what had happened to us. Abuk took my hand and we walked away from the house, away from the others. We found a quiet place and, together, let ourselves cry.

■

I quickly began to hate Turalei. We were targeted by the other kids because we couldn't speak Dinka and because our mother came from a different tribe, making us half-breeds. We were forced to use sign language to indicate to our relatives when we were hungry. Adding to our distress and confusion was our father's disappearance. Again. I was so tired of his vanishing acts and angry that he was leaving us alone with these strangers.

Feeling utterly abandoned, Abuk and I grew even closer. There was no-one else for us to talk to. Abuk took Mama's place, looking after me, making sure I bathed and ate and had a place to sleep. She tried to comfort me, telling me we'd be with Mama again.

Every day, we hoped. One day, Abuk confided in me that she was plotting our escape. I looked up to her and would have done anything she wanted me to do, no matter how crazy. But it wasn't an option. We were terrified by the stories we regularly heard of children being kidnapped and sent to the north and being forced to live as Muslims. We also feared bumping into wild animals along the way.

The other kids continued their cruelty, singing songs that I presumed were mocking us for being half-castes. We hid ourselves in the bushes whenever we could to escape their taunts.

Finally Baba returned from his latest disappearance, only to tell me we were leaving again. Our journey would be much longer this time. I wasn't sorry to be leaving Turalei, but the news came with an even bigger blow—Abuk would not accompany us.

Baba deliberately timed it so we left the house when she wasn't there. I didn't get to say goodbye to my sister. I had adored and trusted Abuk and she had looked after me like she was my mother. When I lost her, I lost the last connection to my previous life.

It seemed heartless, for him to separate the two of us when all we had was each other. It took a long time for me to understand that he had made the right decision. Compared to where we were going, she was in a safer place.

∎

As we walked away from Turalei, Baba carried a five-litre jerry can of water, a sheet that would be our portable bed, and a mosquito net. I carried nothing. I didn't bother asking him why we were leaving Abuk behind. He never answered my questions.

We walked for about three more days just the two of us, not

speaking. I could hear a murmur of voices as we came up to another village. And then I saw the crowd. There must have been thousands of people, and more were coming behind us. I hadn't seen so many people since we'd left Wau. Some of the men were carrying guns, soldiers from the Sudan People's Liberation Army. They were wearing uniforms. I looked up to them and wanted to be as brave as them. There were children my age, too. I was excited to hear some people speaking Arabic, the language I could understand.

The size of the crowd made me assume that we were all here for the same reason. But I didn't know what that was. My frustration with my father was growing. He still hadn't told me where we were going. All he gave me now was a hint of the danger to come.

'We are going on a very long journey, and I want you to keep up with me,' he said. 'You have to be close to me all the time. If you get ahead of me, make sure you stop and wait for me.'

His words frightened me. I wanted to hold his hand but couldn't; his hands were full. I tried to keep close to him, terrified of losing him in the crowd. His long absences had made him a stranger to me, this man that I now depended on for my survival. But I had to trust him.

We were on the move again, but this time we'd walk with the mass of people. It was like a marathon—you start as a huge pack, and then the faster break free and the slower fall behind.

Baba walked very fast, too fast for my little legs. I practically had to run to keep up with him. 'Keep going,' he said when he could tell I was slowing down, stopping only to give me sips of water.

We walked through most of the night, taking advantage of the slight dip in the temperature. It was easier, I figured, to walk when it didn't feel like you were at risk of dissolving in the sun.

I still hadn't got used to sleeping outside. We had been warned of children being snatched by wild animals. We walked quietly, particularly when it was dark, freezing at any rustle from the bush.

The men formed a protective circle, pushing all the children into the centre as we slept. But I was still scared. I lay under my mosquito net, my eyes refusing to close, listening out for the lions in the distance while the men fired their guns to scare them away.

■

The weeks passed in this fashion, descending into a routine that was at once dull and frightening. I had already been a very skinny kid; now, surviving on even less food, I was dangerously thin.

We avoided complete starvation by eating whatever animals we could—we hunted them and they hunted us. We ate anything to avoid becoming one of the skeletal bodies that we regularly came across sprawled on the ground. Baba told me they were just resting, but I didn't believe him. I knew they were dead.

We walked on the hot road in a long single file. Thousands of us. I watched children walking alone. I wondered what had happened to their parents. They appeared lost and frightened as they attached themselves to our long, rambling line.

My feet were scalded and toughened from walking barefoot. The monotony of walking was broken only by the terror of the things that would kill us—the wild animals, the sun that burned with a merciless intensity.

We trekked from village to village, province to province, across southern Sudan.

'When is Abuk coming to meet us?' I tried to ask Baba.

'We'll come back and find her,' he said vaguely.

We came to a village near a river. We had already crossed many streams and rivers, wading through them, the children helped by the grown-ups. But this one was something else. It was vast and deep. I later learnt that it was the great Nile River, which is known as Bahr al Jabal where it flows through southern Sudan.

By now, the thousands of walkers had formed their own smaller groups. Our group comprised about twenty men and boys. I listened to the men debating the best way to cross the river and I stared uneasily at the current rippling through the water. Surely they didn't think we'd be able to swim across that? I watched them talk to a fisherman who had a boat. More and more people arrived after us, until a small crowd had gathered, eyeing the river.

The man must have been persuaded, because soon a group of people ahead of us were getting onto his boat. The current appeared strong, and I overheard people talking about crocodiles in the river. I really didn't want to get on that boat.

I stood and watched warily as the boat began rocking, taking fewer than twenty people at a time. Then it returned and the next group was loaded onto it.

I watched the boat wobble back and forth across the river. Each time, I was convinced it would tip over and its occupants would drown. Miraculously, it didn't, but the whole operation took hours and by the time it was my turn I had worked myself into an anxious mess. I couldn't stop crying. I reasoned that if the boat didn't flip over, then surely the crocodiles would leap onto the boat and eat us. A boy who looked to be my age was using a bucket to rapidly scoop out water. I guessed he was the fisherman's son. That's it, I decided. No-one was making me get on that boat.

When Baba tried to coax me onto the boat I sobbed loudly, stubbornly refusing to move. I could tell he was losing his patience. Two men lifted me and I squirmed in their arms and screamed as they carried me on. Baba held me down as a man began rowing. I couldn't stop moving around, my arms flailing wildly, causing the boat to almost capsize. With each movement the boat rocked and rocked, and Baba couldn't get me to sit still. The others were getting exasperated with the kid who was so hysterical that he might tip over the boat and drown them all. I felt someone knock me on the back of my head and say something in Dinka that I didn't understand. I understood the stern tone, though, and it was enough to make me sit still and look away from the choppy water.

Then stillness. I looked up to see we had made it. We had walked relentlessly for weeks, yet walking had never seemed more appealing. The shoddy river ride must be the worst of it, surely, I thought, as we resumed walking.

I wish I could say that I was right. I wish I'd known where we were going.

It would be weeks more before I was enlightened. We arrived at another village, and Baba told me that we had been trekking east across southern Sudan the whole time, headed for Ethiopia. And the next part of our journey? Walking through the Sahara Desert.

As the war intensified in the mid-1980s and continued to drive people from their homes, tens of thousands of refugees made the long trek from southern Sudan to Ethiopia. The journey covered hundreds of kilometres and was littered with hazards, including a walk through the Sahara Desert. For some, the entire journey took as long as three months.

Many of them were small children who were alone and, left with no other choice, began walking, carrying what little possessions they had. And many didn't make it—starving to death or taken by wild animals along the way.

Other refugees from southern Sudan decided to take their chances in neighbouring Uganda. And some attempted an even more dangerous path—heading to Khartoum in the enemy's territory of northern Sudan, before continuing on to refugee camps in Egypt.

3

Don't Close Your Eyes in the Desert

I stared at my father. He expected me to walk across the Sahara Desert? I didn't even have shoes! All this walking in the sun must have made him lose his senses completely.

But walking across the desert was the only way we could get to Ethiopia and safety. We would be guided by men from the Sudan People's Liberation Army.

I was filled with panic about what we were about to attempt. We bided our time, waiting for the sun to fall. Baba called me over. 'Dip yourself in the river,' he said. I quietly did as he said. I couldn't remember the last time I had had a bath, although I didn't miss the soap that made my eyes sting. That seemed like another world now.

I immersed myself in the water, sucking in as much as I could. 'Drink more. Fill your stomach,' he said.

Baba went to the village and returned with some cow skin. He took each of my blistered feet and placed them on the cow skin, grabbed a knife and cut around my feet until he had fashioned slippers. He tied them to my feet, like flip flops. For the first time in months, I would walk with shoes.

Men were sitting all around in small groups, plotting their desert trek. Some wanted to go quickly and get it over with. Others were more wary, concerned about how the children travelling with them would cope with the desert's harshness.

Baba refilled the five-litre jerry can of water. We needed to carry enough to get us through the desert, but not so much that we were weighed down. Baba estimated it would take a few days.

We made a fire and sat around eating the gazelles the soldiers had hunted and killed. Baba told me to keep eating, even when I was full. I ate until I was stuffed. We had to fill our stomachs because we wouldn't eat for days. There'd be no animals to hunt in the desert.

It was a strange sensation, having a full belly. I hoped it wouldn't be my last meal. I couldn't stop thinking about dying. I was frightened of what the sun would do to us. But my father's presence provided some comfort; surely he wouldn't let me do something that would end in certain death?

We would walk in groups. Most of the others didn't speak Arabic, but by now I had learnt a few words in Dinka. Words like 'come here', 'water', 'don't run', 'walk faster', 'lions', 'crocodiles'. They were simple words—but my survival depended on them.

I made myself brave by convincing myself that I was a soldier. As you prepare for battle, you know that anything can happen to you, that you may lose your life. That's what I imagined our desert walk would be like.

I was lost in my thoughts when one of the men from the army stood up to speak. Maybe he could tell we were frightened. Maybe this was his way of trying to make us feel brave. He told us how well we had done to make it this far. Then the tone of his voice changed to one of hate.

The northern Sudanese—the Arabs, he called them—had taken our homes and killed our people. It was our duty to go to Ethiopia, where we would be trained to be soldiers. We would return to southern Sudan with guns, and drive out the Arabs.

All this time I had thought we were walking to a safer place. But no, we were walking to a place where they would train children to kill.

He told us that the Arabs were the enemy. But I was totally confused. I thought of my wealthier neighbours in Wau. They had come from the north, but they had been kind to me. I remembered how much I had envied their shoes, and their school uniforms. I thought of all the times they had let me share meals with them. They had not seemed evil at all.

Then I thought about our last few months in Wau, and how everything had changed—the end of play, the houses that were burnt to the ground, the smell of the dead bodies in our street. And I thought of Mama, tears running down her face as my father pushed Abuk and me towards the door.

I was persuaded that the man was right. I had to be an eight-year-old man now. The suffering we had gone through had been necessary to give me the strength I needed to return to southern Sudan and fight.

He knew exactly what words to use to make young boys, tired and terrified, do what he wanted us to do. The seed of hatred had been planted.

'Have the courage to keep going,' the man continued. 'In Ethiopia you will have food, and guns, and you will go to school.'

I felt energised. I wanted to walk quickly. I wanted to leave immediately.

I looked around at the other boys, whose faces bore similar looks of determination. The man's speech had had the same impact on them. We were little boys who had become instant men.

As the sun began to set, the men decided it was time. I put on my cow skin flip-flops. We wished each other good luck. See you on the other side.

It was almost dark as we left the village, but the heat was still intense. It was like when you open a hot oven and the heat rushes out and hits you in the face. As we walked further away from the village, the trees became sparser and we were blinded by the setting sun.

We aimed to cover a lot of ground on our first night, while we still had energy and plenty of water. It was our best chance of making it.

We walked in silence. Baba carried the five-litre jerry can of water. I could see the worry etched on his face, and on the faces of all the other men. When we had commenced our journey, Baba had been relaxed about letting me walk a little behind him. But now he insisted that I always walk in front of him where he could see me. If I fell behind even a little, he would place his hand on the top of my back and push me ahead of him.

I could see bodies strewn across the sand. There were so many. It seemed that you'd walk just a few hundred metres and come across more bodies. From a distance, I could pretend they were resting. But as we moved closer, I could tell they were dead. They must have gone on the same desperate journey as us—they had defied guns, wild animals and starvation. But they couldn't defeat the desert.

I couldn't feel anything. I had seen dead bodies before, and I sensed this wouldn't be the last time. My father looked at me in concern, expecting me to be shocked and sickened. But I met his gaze calmly, expressionless. Death had become normal to me.

The first time I had seen dead bodies was in Wau. One morning, Mama and I walked out of our home to the shocking scene of huts burnt to the ground. Enmeshed in the charred debris were bodies, including children lying beside their mothers.

Mama had quickly steered us back into the house. But I'd seen enough. I didn't sleep that night and for many nights after. Each night I'd lie awake, waiting for the men with guns to storm into our home. In the morning, sometimes we'd notice more dead people. That's when the exodus from Wau began. They left—like Baba and Abuk and me—abruptly. I didn't get to say goodbye to my friends. I have never seen them again. I don't know if they're alive.

I didn't cry for the dead bodies now. Baba must have thought he was doing me a favour by telling me they were people who were tired and resting. I let him think that I believed him.

I wanted to run the entire length of the desert to get the whole thing over and done with. I tried to be brave. But there were moments when all I wanted to do was stop, fall into a heap in the sand and indulge myself with a long cry. Baba kept me motivated by appealing to my competitive instincts. 'Look, the other kids your age are walking right past you. Look at that little boy walking faster than you!' he scolded.

Most of my pain was concentrated in my feet; they were hot and aching. At one point, the cloth that Baba had used to tie the flip-flop on one foot broke, and the edges began rubbing against the side of my foot until it was bleeding. It stung like hell. And that's when I remembered my first-aid kit. I stopped walking and peed on my foot.

■

We continued walking all night. With darkness our only shade, it was the best time. We stopped to rest only as the sun emerged. Baba mended my shoes so they would no longer cause me pain. I hadn't slept all night, but still I could appreciate the beautiful sunrise over the endless sand.

The sun brought instant stifling heat. We searched for a spot to rest and hide. But seeking shade was futile in the desert.

Baba checked our water and made the worrying discovery that we had already gone through half of it. We still had two days of walking to go. From then on he carefully controlled our supplies. When I told him I was thirsty, he'd let me have only a sip.

As others ran out of their supplies, we resorted to hiding what little we had left. They'd stagger over to us and drop to their knees, their faces desperate. 'Please, give me some water,' they pleaded. I could tell that Baba felt bad about it, but he couldn't give them our water. He hid the jerry can inside the mosquito net and sheet that he had tied to his back, guarding it like a precious jewel.

When we couldn't walk any more, Baba took out his sheet. He held up one end and another man held up the other. The children slid into the middle, and the men held the sheet over our heads and theirs. This was our only shade. The first time, I almost drifted off to sleep, but Baba wouldn't let me. 'You can't close your eyes in the desert,' he said. To close your eyes was to summon death.

The fear of dying in the desert kept me awake. I didn't want to die in the desert. If I was going to die, I wanted to die as a heroic soldier. Each time we stopped to rest, I watched men slouch onto the sand and wearily close their eyes. You could tell the fight was rapidly leaving their bodies. Each time we resumed our walk, there was almost always someone left behind.

■

We walked all through the second night. It was Baba who broke the silence.

'Let's sit down and rest,' he said tiredly.

I was immediately alarmed. It was unlike him to suggest that we rest while it was dark. The shade of darkness was our best walking time.

He sat on the sand, unpacked the water, and gestured to me to take it. 'Drink this water now, or carry it with you. If anyone asks you for water, don't give it to them. I'll follow you soon.'

His eyelids began to droop and I remembered what he'd said about closing your eyes in the desert. I panicked that it would be the end of him.

I sat beside him, wondering what to do. I had to make sure that he didn't close his eyes.

'It's OK, I'm just resting for a little while,' he said. 'I'll be behind you.'

'No. You rest, and then we'll go together,' I said.

He tried to close his eyes again. I grabbed his shoulder and shook him urgently. 'I'm awake,' he mumbled, opening his eyes briefly and then closing them again.

I kept shaking him. 'Baba, drink the water!'

'No, it's for you,' he said.

'Baba, you drink it,' I said. He wouldn't. I pushed the jerry can to his mouth. He opened his parched lips and let me dribble the last of the water into his mouth. I sighed with relief.

We stayed there for about an hour more, waiting for Baba to regain some energy. I wondered whether, with that last mouthful of water, I had saved his life.

■

Even when the sun emerged we didn't stop walking. I tried to shrug off the sun's intensity by thinking about what I would do once we were in Ethiopia.

I looked hard into the distance. For the first time I could see something. I couldn't make out what the blur of dark objects was. It was the first time in days I had seen anything other than sand and sun and sky.

We walked towards the dark objects, straining our eyes. And then Baba pointed to the dark shapes. 'See that? They're trees!' he said. 'That's where we're going!'

Trees! That meant our desert walk was almost over. I felt a sudden surge of energy. I wanted to run to the trees and roll around in their shade. But we still had a long way to go.

For hours, the trees kept our spirits up. Even the sun didn't stop us. As we drew closer, a faint glistening captured our attention—something that looked like water!

We ran with surprising vigour towards it. It was kind of like a small pond. We paused long enough to notice that it looked dirty. But we were so desperate we didn't care. We jumped in and greedily sucked in mouthfuls.

No-one talked, concentrating on drinking the filthy liquid. After a few minutes I raised my head, and was sickened by what I saw.

'Baba, look!' I shouted, pointing.

The bodies appeared to have been there for a long time. The others kept drinking, oblivious to what I had seen. By now, more people had arrived and jumped—like we had—jubilantly into the dirty water.

Baba surveyed the scene and pulled me away. 'Can you vomit?' he said.

I shook my head. He walked away and I watched him force himself to vomit, wishing I could do the same.

For those who died there, the combination of the dirty water and the exhaustion must have taken their toll. Some were probably so dehydrated that they were beyond the point of being saved. I watched people drink the water, satisfied, and then sit beneath a tree, closing their eyes—never to open them again. It was unbearably sad to me that they had survived such a gruelling journey, only to die at the very end of it.

I was convinced the dirty water would be the end of me, too. People were vomiting all over the place. One man was trying to stop those still arriving from drinking. 'Please don't drink the water, you'll get sick. You'll die,' he pleaded.

But severe dehydration makes you desperate. They ignored him. I watched helplessly as more people swallowed the dirty water. I watched a man kneel down and scoop handfuls of it into his mouth, then fall face down into it.

I couldn't bear to watch any more. I drifted away and found a place beneath a tree. I thought it was just a matter of time before I passed out. If I was going to die, it might as well be in a shady spot.

I must have fallen asleep. I opened my eyes, which were fuzzy from sleep. I was still alive.

I was so hungry. I went looking for my father and found him lying on the ground with his eyes closed. I shook him until he woke. 'I'm hungry,' I said.

He went over to a man who was holding a gun, and asked him where we could find food. The man looked around, saw a wild animal grazing nearby, pointed his gun, and shot it. 'There you go, there's food,' he said.

Baba told me not to eat too much, just a little bit now, slowly, and more later. The combined stench of dead bodies and vomit quickly banished my appetite. I chewed on a small piece of meat but couldn't finish it. I sat there, waiting to die like the others.

We still had no water. But there was no way we were going to drink from the dirty pond again. We needed a river.

We summoned the energy for a few more hours of walking until we found one. Relieved, we jumped in. Afterwards, we sat beneath a tree as more and more survivors arrived. We had covered hundreds of kilometres over three months. And we had made it. So many of our friends hadn't. We sat together, eating the meat of the animals we had killed, enjoying a rare moment of peace.

We lit a fire and sat around it as it grew dark, nervously listening to the lions in the distance. I lay near the fire, sharing a sheet with two other boys. I wondered if the lions found little boys tasty for dinner. The three of us each wanted to be the boy that slept in the middle. It was the best spot, we reasoned, because the lions would snatch the boys sleeping on the ends first.

I was the quickest, and jumped in the middle. We lay there together quietly until one of the boys thought I had fallen asleep. Then he shoved me aside, taking my place in the middle. He thought he was being clever, but I knew what he was up to. I waited for him to fall asleep, then pushed him aside and reclaimed my position. The three of us played this game all night, too frightened to sleep.

■

We inched closer to Ethiopia. One day we noticed scores of people lying on the ground beneath a tree, faces pained, crying, vomiting. A man told us they had inadvertently eaten poisonous fruit that they had picked from the tree.

We wondered how we could stop others from eating the fruit. We couldn't write a sign, as so many people couldn't read. One of the men used a machete to cut the tree down. Then we set it on fire.

A few days later we arrived in Pochalla. From here, it was just a few days' walk to Ethiopia. Men from the Sudan People's Liberation Army were all over the place. They looked so striking in their uniforms. I wanted to be one of them.

They told us that once we got to the camp, there would be plenty of food. The children would get to go to school. There would be opportunities to be trained, to learn how to use a gun, before we returned to southern Sudan to fight.

I wanted a gun so badly. I wanted to kill as many Arabs from the north as I could.

*Exhausted, starving, and lucky to be alive, those who made it to
Ethiopia ended up in one of three camps: Pinyudo, Dimma or
Itang. It was 1987, and there were whole families in the camps,
separated from the children who had come alone.*

*The refugees in the three camps exceeded one hundred
thousand, and most of them came from the Dinka and Nuer tribes,
whose men were strongly represented in the rebel movement.
They gave the appearance of being refugee camps, although it
was a long time before the aid arrived. And the Sudan People's
Liberation Amy (SPLA) was in control.*

*There were fiery clashes with the local Anuak people who
lived near the Pinyudo camp. Meanwhile in Sudan, the change in
leadership had not brought peace—despite the commencement of
talks between the SPLA and Prime Minister Sadiq al-Mahdi.*

4

Welcome to Ethiopia, Welcome to Hell

We crossed the invisible line separating our countries and entered Ethiopia. Baba and I were sent to a place called Pinyudo camp. I looked around, searching for the white people who were meant to be here to help us, and the mountains of food we had been told about. I had expected a thriving camp with a school and houses. All I saw was a giant space filled with nothing.

I felt deceived. We had come all this way, and there was barely any food. The camp leaders gave us machetes and pointed to the trees and told us to build our own huts in which to sleep. Our roofs were plastic sheets to keep the rain out.

I rarely saw my father. Baba lost ownership of me the moment we entered Pinyudo. The camp leaders owned me now. If I wanted to see Baba, I had to get permission. There were girls in the camp, too, in a separate area, mostly living with their families. We didn't see much of them. I was glad now that Mama and my sisters had stayed in Sudan. I couldn't bear the thought of them being in this horrible place. I wondered whether they were alive, and how Abuk was coping with the kids who had been cruel to us in Turalei.

The camp leaders called us 'comrade' or '*jaysh ahmar*'—'red army'. I felt that they chose these words very deliberately, to remind us this was no holiday—we were here to be groomed as soldiers.

The place was surrounded by a huge fence to keep us in and the hostile locals, the Anuak people, out. It was quite military—you could barely do anything without permission. It felt like a detention centre. It felt like hell.

Each morning the screech of a whistle signalled the start of 'parade'—an assembly where we were given our chores and instructions for the day.

The army's presence was palpable. It wasn't hard to find the guns and grenades. I admired the army men and their guns. Sometimes they'd let me help them clean their guns. I became a nine-year-old expert, deftly dismantling the guns and putting them back together.

The camp was soon besieged by a multitude of diseases. I watched people stare death in the face and lose. Malaria was an easy victor over children who were already malnourished, weak and dejected. The river near the camp was rife with crocodiles, and wild animals lurked menacingly nearby.

We wandered around the camp, faces hollowed from hunger. I heard rumours of cannibalism, of famished children so desperate that they ate each other. We looked at each other suspiciously, wondering if we were safe in the huts we shared. I don't know if the rumours were true—I never saw any evidence of it.

I survived in the way I had grown accustomed—by scrambling for whatever food I could get. But as one of the youngest kids in the camp, it was a regular fight. They placed us in groups of about ten boys for our one meal of the day. The food was piled onto a large plate, and the boys in each group would wait their turn to take their share. The food was always served very hot. The boys in my group were older than me, and they were sneaky. They turned up with tins or large spoons that they dipped into the plate, giving themselves huge portions. I don't know where they got the tins and spoons. All I had was my hands. By the time it was my turn, the older boys had virtually scraped the plate clean.

One night, I watched the boys turn up with their spoons and tins and knew I'd miss out again. Famished and frustrated, I totally lost it. I grabbed the plate and tipped it over. Maize and beans went flying all over the place but I didn't care—if I couldn't eat, the other boys wouldn't either.

They were so mad, diving on me and taking it in turns to belt me, making me cry through my hunger. The commotion caught the attention of one of the respected men in the camp, a man named Pieng. '*Jaysh ahmar*, what's going on?' he asked. 'Why did you tip over the food?'

I told him that I felt hungry every day. I told him about the older boys and their tins and big spoons. He listened to my whining, and called over the man in charge of feeding us.

He told him to group the boys together based on their age, so the oldest were together, and the youngest. He told him to wait for the food to cool down before serving it, and to make sure all the boys had an equal portion, so that no-one went hungry.

Then he grabbed my hand. 'Come with me,' he said. 'What's your name?'

I was thrilled. This nice, important man was talking to me! I smirked at the others. I hoped they were jealous.

He took me to his hut and let me eat with him. He made me feel more human than I had felt in a long time. Pieng helped a lot of us boys, and actually took the time to talk to us. He was someone we looked up to. In the absence of our parents, he was like our father.

■

There was a river near the camp where crocodiles lived. One of my chores was to fetch water for cooking. We were allowed to swim in the river, but I didn't know how to swim. The river was very deep and I was afraid. At first I hung around the edge and the boys teased me for swimming on the girls' end.

On the other side of the river, away from our camp, tall mango trees belonging to the locals flourished. I loved mangoes. I thought they might help satisfy the perpetual emptiness in my belly. It killed me that I couldn't swim across the river, climb the trees and devour the mangoes.

Over the weeks, the mangoes became a fixation. I knew there was only one way I was going to get to them. I'd have to teach myself how to swim. So when summer came, I forced myself to get over the fear. Tentatively at first, I pulled away from the edge until I gained the confidence to enter deeper water. I taught myself to float, to balance myself in the water. Right—it was mango time.

I rounded up the boys. Just as I had encouraged my friends to climb the electricity poles in Wau, I remained a natural leader stirring up trouble. We jumped into the river and effortlessly swam to our goal. We climbed the trees with ease, perched on the branches and happily helped ourselves to the mangoes. The sweet fruit dribbled down our faces.

It had been so easy that we returned repeatedly over the weeks. It really pissed off the locals. We got into a routine. You'd climb a tree, choose a branch and own it for the rest of the day. We were spread out amongst the trees one day, stuffing ourselves with mangoes. And then we heard gunshots and froze.

A local man had seen us, and he wasn't happy. He cocked his gun and began shooting into the air.

We sat on our branches, panicking. He hadn't hit any of us. I couldn't tell if that was deliberate, or if he just had terrible aim. Either way, I wasn't sticking around to find out.

'There's no time to climb down!' I screamed at the others. 'Jump into the river!'

We flew like birds, diving off our branches and into the river, the sound of gunshots still in our ears, swimming underwater to safety. We all made it—except for one of our friends. In panic, he had miscalculated the jump and landed awkwardly on the ground. He lay there groaning and crying. He couldn't move, let alone run.

From the other side of the river, we fearfully watched the man standing over our friend, holding his gun. We didn't know what to do.

And then he walked away, leaving our friend squirming in agony, and we swam back to him in relief. I could see something pointy jutting out of the boy's thigh. We picked him up and, between a few of us, solemnly carried him across the river back to camp.

He was taken to a hospital in Addis Ababa, where he stayed for a while. When he returned to camp he was limping. A metal plate had been inserted into his leg. Still, he continued to play with us. We called him 'Iron Man'. We'd say: 'Hey, you have to be in this guy's team because that is not a human leg!'

■

We tried to extract what little enjoyment we could from the hell of our lives in Pinyudo. We made fun where there was no fun. We formed a family where there was no family.

Indulging any feelings of depression could kill you here. I watched boys die because they gave in to their misery. Their longing for their parents was so unbearable that they isolated themselves and gave up. Dying became preferable to the longing, so they refused what little food we had and they didn't fight when the diseases came to take them.

We were so hungry that many of us boys went looting in the homes of the local Anuak people. We far outnumbered the locals in the village. In one particularly nasty clash, we drove them out of their homes. Houses were burnt down as we stole whatever food we could eat. People on both sides were killed. But we were desperate. We would do anything to eat, and to survive.

I vowed not to let anything I saw break me. I locked away the images of the dead bodies in my head and didn't give myself permission to dwell on them. Not even the tiny insects that drove us all crazy—by somehow embedding themselves beneath your skin and laying eggs—would get to me. Even when they itched like hell. I became so good at extracting them that the boys would form a queue for my help.

Having a laugh was the only way I could imagine emerging from this hell. But the locals made it hard. We were the unwanted guests playing on their turf. They plotted ways to hurt us.

The riverbank near our camp had a sloping part that we used as a slide. When we were free from our chores we'd slide down the grass and jump into the river. Whoever made the biggest splash was the winner. We were at it for hours during the summer months.

One afternoon, we came out running, each wanting to be the first boy to slide in. One of the boys broke free of the rest of us, stripped off his clothes, ran ahead and slid down the slope and into the water.

I saw the blood before I heard him howl in pain. We all stopped, panting, staring at the riverbank in amazement. Some of the locals had planted razor blades in the mud. As our friend had slid down the slope, the razors had cut his naked body. His buttocks were bleeding.

We longed for revenge. I was determined to continue eating their mangoes, even when things got ugly and the other boys chickened out. I'd swim across the river, pick as many mangoes as I could carry, and take them back to the others.

One day, a few of us swam across. The smell of cooking meat emanated from one of the houses. My belly rumbled. No-one was home. We broke in and helped ourselves, devouring the whole thing, then quickly bailed. We didn't even get busted.

Our camp was near a village with lots of live chickens that belonged to the locals. Sometimes, the chickens would venture close enough to our camp for us to capture and kill them. Most of the boys at Pinyudo camp had boring food or hardly any food. But for a little while, my friends and I had chicken.

We plotted ways to steal the chickens at night and kill them. Sometimes we'd grab a chicken and break its neck. Sometimes I would crawl beneath the camp fence and sneak into the village. I had made a new sling from two branches joined together to make a v-shape. Attached to the branches was a piece of elastic cut off from the inner tube of an old bicycle. My friend got the broken tube from a local, in exchange for his T-shirt.

Making the sling had brought on a wave of homesickness. It reminded me of my Uncle Fadul and Mama and home. My uncle had taught me well. I aimed and fired and easily hit my target.

But we had been careless; we left a trail of chicken bones. The elders at the camp began asking questions about where the bones had come from. The other boys dobbed me in. I had, after all, initiated the chicken stealing. I pointed out that the others had enjoyed the chicken as much as I had. Still, I confessed, and I was punished.

Using a cane, they gave my bare buttocks twenty lashes. My bum was red and bleeding by the end and I was in agony. If that wasn't bad enough, they made me stand in the sun for two hours—bare-arsed. It was even worse than the punishment Mama used to give me.

We stopped stealing chickens after that. By then, we were rapidly running out of ways to amuse ourselves. We tried to go back to our river slide, carefully looking out for razors planted in the grass. But the locals had found an even more effective way to hurt us. One day, a boy went flying down the slope and into the river and screamed. The fleshy part of his leg had been pierced by a spear. He was very lucky— it could have been a vital organ. It turned out that some locals had planted spears in the water. The riverbank was closed off completely after that.

■

The pile of starved and diseased bodies continued to grow inside Pinyudo. And then a deadly outbreak of cholera raced through the camp. Looking back, it was hardly a surprise. We were living in dirty, unhygienic conditions.

By then, I'd lost count of the dead bodies I'd seen. Most parents try to protect their children from such horrendous images. Not us. We were little boys who carried the daunting duty of burying our own friends.

The first friend I buried was Mach. I'm not even sure what killed him in the end; there was so much disease around, it wasn't uncommon for a boy to be infected by more than one at a time. Three of us wrapped his stricken body in a blanket and carried it to a makeshift cemetery, where we dug his grave and buried him. I couldn't sleep after that first time.

As the number of daily burials grew, I came to dread the mornings because I knew what my first unpleasant chore for the day would be. We used shovels to dig the graves. But being so young and weak from hunger, we didn't have the strength to bury their bodies properly. Our innocent carelessness was punished. The next morning, we'd find that hyenas and lions had dug up the graves, and bits of the bodies were scattered everywhere. That was even more traumatic than the deaths themselves.

The camp leaders tried to reduce the deaths by isolating the sickest in a hut together. One day, I was sick enough to be one of them.

I was placed in isolation with eight other boys. There were no health workers at this stage, I wasn't aware of any medicine, and there was no-one to look after us.

I had been in isolation for around a week. I was beginning to feel slightly better, and I went outside one morning to brush my teeth. My toothbrush was a stick, with one end chewed off to soften it.

I expected the other sick boys to soon follow, as they had every other morning. I hung around outside for a while, waiting for them to wake up. I thought they must still be asleep. I decided to be their alarm clock. One by one, I tried to shake each boy awake. 'Come on guys, wake up, the sun is shining,' I shouted.

They didn't stir. I was the only boy in the hut to have survived the night. I ran outside screaming over and over: 'I don't want to be isolated anymore! I don't want to die! Please let me come out!'

Later, I sadly helped to bury my friends' emaciated bodies, wondering why I hadn't died with them.

■

Isolation wasn't working. The leaders decided they had to be more proactive to eradicate disease. They said that we were getting sick and dying because we were living in dirty conditions. We had no proper toilets. Whenever someone wanted to do a number two, they went anywhere. Any spot in a bush. When it rained, the faeces washed into the water—the same water we used for drinking, for cooking and washing our dishes. No wonder we were getting sick.

The leaders set up an area far from where we slept specifically for doing number twos. This was fine during the day. But at night, when we could hear the wild animals in the darkness, it was really scary. So when it was dark, instead of walking to the place where you were supposed to do your number twos, many boys ignored the rules and went anywhere.

The camp leaders weren't happy. They appointed men to act as night security watch—kind of like the Poo Police. Their job was to make sure you did your number twos where you were meant to. Any boy busted doing an illegal number two would be punished.

I wasn't deterred. The prospect of meeting wild animals in the darkness was more frightening. So I took my chances with the Poo Police. Besides, I thought one night as I dropped my shorts, it's too dark for them to see me.

I was crouching in the bushes not too far from my hut. The Poo Police were polite enough to wait for me to finish before they pounced. The moment I stood up and began pulling up my shorts, about six guys rounded on me and began beating me. Six men!

'Pick it up,' one of them snapped while the beating continued. Was he kidding? None of the men were smiling.

I wasn't even allowed to use anything. I screwed up my nose to avoid smelling it, and with trembling bare hands picked up my own faeces. It was soft to the touch. I gagged and tried not to throw up. They marched me to a place where I could dispose of the faeces. But it wasn't over.

The Poo Police marched me to another area filled with the illegal number twos belonging to other boys. Some of it was old and hard, and some of it was disturbingly fresh. They made me clean up the mess, using my bare hands again. I gagged the whole time.

I was scarred by the experience for weeks. Word of my misadventure got around the camp, and I was thoroughly shamed. I declined involvement with all camp activities for a while, preferring to stay inside the hut I shared with the other boys, withdrawing from everyone.

While the refugees tried to settle and cope with their bleak existence in the Ethiopian camps, southern Sudan remained under fire. Government troops continued their attacks on villages and there were reports of human rights abuses and slavery. More refugees steadily continued to cross the border into Ethiopia.

Men from the Sudan People's Liberation Army visited the boys in the camps, stirring them with speeches and songs.

Omar al-Bashir came to power in 1989, in a coup that threw out Prime Minister Sadiq al-Mahdi. He operated under the banner of the Revolutionary Command Council for National Salvation. The move effectively stalled any talks of peace with the SPLA for some time.

5

The Beautiful Game

It took a while, but the world finally heard we were here. Then the aid workers came. And the food. There were giant white bags, labelled 'sorghum' in red. I hadn't eaten sorghum in ages. I was so excited to see the bland grain that I used to eat daily in Wau. It reminded me of home and Mama's cooking.

We had medicine too. I was mad that it had taken so long. I thought of all the bodies I had buried, and the people who might have been saved if we'd had doctors and proper medical supplies earlier. It was an obscene waste.

Someone, probably from the Office of the United Nations High Commissioner for Refugees, asked me how old I was. I told them that I didn't know. I had never celebrated a birthday in my life. It was a common thing in Sudan; children often had no birth certificate, and so many people were illiterate. Parents instead remembered their children's year of birth by associating it with a major event, such as a year of starvation, or a year someone special died. Age is a big thing in the West but for us, not knowing how old we were was no big deal. I guess we had so much more to worry about.

Many of us didn't know our birthdays. So they gave us the same birthday—1 January. The white people looked at me closely and estimated that I was born in 1983. That would have made me about five. I didn't argue with them, and the apparent year of my birth stuck.

More than thirty years of my life went by before I learnt my true age. I was so small that they had underestimated my age by five years.

There were regular white visitors to the camp now. My good friend Emmanuel and I were trained to speak to them. Emmanuel and I had hit it off immediately. When we met, I recognised his cheekiness because it mirrored mine. I thought we'd get along just fine. We climbed the mango trees together. He was the boy I slept beside in the hut we shared with some other boys.

Even as little boys, we learnt to tell our stories. To the other kids we were like mini-celebrities in the camp because we often talked to the white people. We called the white people '*kawaja*'. They asked us: How is life in the camp? What food do you eat? What do you need? 'We need food, clean water, we want to go to school,' we told them.

As a reward for talking to them, we were permitted to go to a makeshift store and choose clothes. I'd pick a couple of things and would be about to leave when Emmanuel would say, 'Hey, what are you doing? Take some more!' So I would.

One of the *kawaja* took a photo of Emmanuel and me as we spoke to them. It was the first time I'd seen a camera. I was given a copy of the photo of us—two skinny kids who had forged a friendship out of war. I kept the photo with my modest possessions.

I felt that talking to the *kawaja* was a big responsibility. We were representing other boys in the camp and what we said really mattered. The SPLA told us not to tell the aid workers about the children who were being sent away for soldier training. I kept the secret.

■

Life in Pinyudo gradually became more bearable. We got a school. My father, being an educated man, was one of the teachers. I still wasn't seeing much of him but considered myself luckier than most of the other kids. At least I knew my father was alive. Many others had been orphaned or separated from their parents while escaping Sudan.

Our classroom was the shade of a tree. Sitting beneath the tree, I learnt to write for the first time. I loved it. But I struggled to write the figure '8'. The curves confused me. One of my teachers found an effective way to help me get it right. He grabbed my fingers and pressed them down onto the ground, making me trace the figure 8 over and over, demanding to know why I couldn't do it properly. We went through this so many times that my fingers almost bled. But it worked. I now have a perfectly formed 8.

We had the choice of learning in English or Arabic. Being exposed to the white people in the camp had taught me that English was a more useful language. I had also figured out that having an education would get me very far. It could even be the key to a different life.

A charity had donated exercise books, but there weren't enough of them. The teachers cut them in half so that more could go around. We were hungry for education, and when a boy lost his book he'd steal another boy's. I guarded mine fiercely. To lose my book would have meant losing my ability to learn. Each night, I tucked my book inside my shirt as I slept.

We were also each given half a pencil and an eraser. I clung to my three precious possessions—my book, pencil and eraser—and carried them everywhere.

I competed shamelessly with the other kids. We played a spelling game, where we sat in a circle and the first boy would have to think of a word. He would write down the first letter of the word, and the next boy would have to guess the next letter and write it down, and on it would go. The boy who guessed the final letter would have to pronounce the word and explain its meaning. Boys lost points for not knowing a letter or a word.

Being naturally competitive, I excelled at this game. I spent a lot of time dreaming up words to make it harder for the other boys. I wanted them to lose. I knew their weakness was words beginning with z, x and q. I asked the teachers to teach me words that started with these letters. I became so notorious that the other boys dreaded playing the word game with me.

Faith had become really important to me, and another tree in a different part of the camp was our church. Praying became a routine that I depended on; having faith seemed to be my only escape. Without faith, I felt that I wouldn't survive.

Nuns arrived from Italy, bringing robes and rosaries for us. There was a priest who had made the trek from Sudan with us. We called him Abuna Madol. Abuna means 'priest'. Because of the war, many of us had still not been baptised. Up until now, I had gone by the name Nyuol. When you're baptised, you get a new name. With a priest at the camp, this was our chance.

First, in the absence of our parents, we each had to pick a name. I found the whole experience deeply disturbing. I couldn't think of a name. Abuna Madol gave us some ideas. If you're finding it hard, he said, why don't you choose a name beginning with the first letter of the name you already have? For instance, he said I could draw on the 'N' for Nyuol to be Nicholas.

So I half-heartedly told Abuna Madol I would be Nicholas. Still, it didn't sound right. We were due to be baptised the next day, and I still hadn't thought of a name. I was so frustrated that I lay beneath a tree, isolating myself, thinking hard.

This next bit sounds really corny, but I swear it happened. I began praying to God. I said: 'God, show me a sign if you are really there.' I fell asleep, still uninspired and nameless. I woke up a few hours later. The name 'David' had popped into my head, like someone was shouting it at me. I know it sounds ridiculous, but it's true.

I told Abuna Madol the story, and he laughed out loud at me. Still, I was baptised that day, and David became my name.

■

I loved Abuna Madol and was keen to get involved with the church. I became an altar boy, which was considered a great privilege. The job came with other benefits—being so important made the girls want to talk to you. We didn't get to see the girls in the camp much. Going to church was one of the rare occasions that we did. It was through church, when I was about ten, that I fell in love for the first time.

She was a good runner, and taller than me. Her name was Achol, and she was so pretty. I made sure that I sat beside her in the church choir whenever I could. I wanted to be near her. I wondered if she felt the same. We'd often sit together, talking and giggling.

I had to tell her how I felt. But I didn't have the courage to tell her to her face. I decided to write her a letter. I knew it was a risk, because such letters—and any romantic sentiments at all—were forbidden in the camp. My position as an altar boy made it particularly risky. For true love, though, I felt it was a risk worth taking.

Using my basic English, I constructed simple sentences. I decided to give her the letter at church the following day. I put the letter in the pocket of my pants, where I thought it would be safe.

But as the day went on, I lost my nerve. I decided against declaring myself. I took off my pants and changed into a pair of shorts to play. I wanted to keep my pants nice.

My friend came out to play too, and put on my discarded pants. It wasn't unusual for us to share clothes and I wasn't fussed about it. I had forgotten all about my amorous efforts of earlier in the day.

Sunday morning came, and it was my turn to be an altar boy. I put on my robe and went about my usual chores, sweeping clean the area beneath the tree that was our church. Just before the service was due to start, Abuna Madol came to me and said: 'Take off the robe.' I did as I was told. 'Go and call another boy to take your place,' he said. 'You won't be an altar boy today.'

I was baffled. We always took it in turns to be altar boys, and today was meant to be my turn. I sat down with the others, my head ticking over with worry. I had no idea what was going on.

After the service, Abuna Madol instructed one of the boys, Victor, to go and get a cane. 'David, come here,' he said.

There would have been hundreds of people there. I stood up in front of everyone. I had carefully done my hair and worn the best clothes I could find, because I knew Achol would be there.

'I always tell you things, and you don't listen,' he began. 'Especially when you're as young as David and you write letters you aren't supposed to.'

Oh God, the letter! It had totally slipped my mind. The letter must have fallen out of my friend's pocket as we played, and ended up in the wrong hands. Now that Abuna Madol had brought it up, my heart was beating fast. He produced the letter from his pocket and began reading it aloud. Achol burst into tears when she heard her name.

I'd like to think her tears were for me, but I doubt it. All the others were laughing at me. I stood there quietly, sweating, only once daring to look at her.

My punishment was twenty straps administered in front of the whole congregation. I saw one of the sisters stand up and walk out, unable to bring herself to watch what was going to happen next.

I stood my ground, wincing, stung by the public humiliation. I didn't feel the pain of the cane. I looked straight ahead during every lash. I did not cry.

The next part of my punishment was to kneel and pray for several hours. I wasn't supposed to eat but a sister found some food and secretly gave it to me while Abuna Madol was napping. I wanted to punish myself for being such an idiot. So I shaved off my curly afro hair. I don't know why, but it made me feel better.

Nothing was going to happen with Achol after that. She later found me and unleashed her fury. She told me I was crazy, and not to ever do it again.

I have no ill will towards Abuna Madol for literally beating the love out of a little boy. I understand why he did it, why he had to make an example of his altar boy.

■

I found another way to escape the despair of the camp: I immersed myself in soccer. The older boys in the camp had already been playing the game in Sudan, but I'd never seen it before. I spent hours watching them play, totally inspired by their skill.

When I tried to copy them, I found that I was naturally really good at it. Only the big boys had soccer balls. So I found a sock and stuffed it with paper and cloth and whatever rubbish I could find until it was round. It was a socker ball.

I think it must have been a means of escape for all of us, because soccer's popularity quickly grew in the camp. It was the only good thing we had. We crafted a pitch by cutting down the trees, pulling out their roots and smoothing the ground with our hands.

I played for hours with Emmanuel and some other boys, until my feet hurt. Sometimes I played too hard, kicking the rocks instead of the ball. One time I almost broke my toe and couldn't play for a couple of weeks. I was frantic. I wanted to get back to playing.

We formed teams and started a real competition inside the camp. But only the older boys were allowed to play at that level. My favourite team were called Group Two, and they were the champions. I admired the captain, a talented striker named Lueth. Crowds from inside the camp gathered to watch and cheered wildly when a boy scored. I'd never seen anything like it in my life. Still, I instinctively knew how to play. And I wanted to play with the big boys.

There was a man, Madong, who was in charge of the camp sports. He would sometimes watch the little boys play. I had practised really hard and I was very good. It was like the socker ball was attached to my foot. No-one could take it away from me. 'What's your name?' Madong said one day. 'When you grow up, you will become a famous soccer player.' I was thrilled at the praise.

Madong asked me if I wanted to play with the older boys. I started out as their ball boy. They let me eat with them, and I happily cleaned their shoes and washed their socks. I would have done anything for them.

During the games, I stood to the side and watched, rapt. And one day, I got my chance. Near the end of one match, Lueth began walking towards me, pulling off his shirt.

'Hey, put this on!' he shouted. I grinned madly. The crowd cheered as they watched the little kid pull on Lueth's sweaty shirt.

There were only a few minutes remaining. I was so intimidated by the crowd, and I don't know how I found my confidence. A teammate passed the ball to me and I ran, dribbling the ball between my feet. My opponents were much bigger than me, but I outsmarted them. The crowd pointed and laughed at the little boy easily outrunning and outmanoeuvring the bigger boys. It was hilarious.

I didn't score, but that wasn't really the point. My role wasn't to score, but to entertain. The match had already been won. When the game was over, my teammates picked me up and the crowd roared in appreciation. I became quite a character in the camp after that. Unbeknown to me, excelling at soccer would give me extra protection inside Pinyudo.

After my debut, I became a regular fixture in the games. As a match drew to its conclusion, the crowd would chant my name, wanting to see the spectacle of the kid taking on the big boys. When I played, it was comedy time.

Losses were rare for us. We suffered only the odd loss to teams that weren't as good as ours. It's like when Manchester City beats Manchester United—it's a huge blow and everyone is in shock.

It had taken a while, but I had found a purpose. I directed all my energy into school and soccer. In doing so, I could almost pretend that I wasn't living in hell. I could indulge the fantasy that I was a normal boy getting an education and playing soccer after school. I carried my exercise book and my soccer ball with me everywhere, like symbols of hope for a future I could only dream of.

■

The boys at the other camps played soccer as well and there was a competition between all the camps. The boys from our camp were to travel to Itang to play a team there. The best players from Pinyudo were chosen to go. I wasn't left out of the team.

Our team piled onto the back of a truck for the long drive to Itang. It was my first time ever in a vehicle. On the way, we stopped in a town called Gambela. We walked into a real restaurant with tables and chairs. I had never been inside a restaurant before. We sat down and I looked around, fascinated.

Someone placed a bottle of Coke in front of me. I stared at it curiously. I had no idea what it was. It must be alcohol, I thought. I'd better not drink it. I didn't want to get smashed before such an important contest.

The other boys were guzzling their Coke. I asked whether it was OK for me to drink it. They laughed. 'Go ahead, it's not alcohol,' they said.

I took a swig. The first gulp made me cough and choke as the overwhelming sensation of gas and sugar hit me. It may as well have been booze. The others laughed at me again. I took small sips. I couldn't manage more.

It was a day of firsts—first car, first restaurant, first fizzy drink. And tonight, we were staying in a hotel! I couldn't believe it. I had spent months walking across southern Sudan, I had trekked through a desert, I had watched people die and then buried their bodies. And now, I would sleep in a hotel!

I began to think about what had got me to this moment—being good at soccer and talking to white people. And I understood that if I continued to be good at soccer and talking to white people, the opportunities to change my life would come.

We arrived at Itang camp, and the team debated whether I should get some time on the pitch. They worried it would be too dangerous for me. Our opponents at Pinyudo camp might have indulged me because I was such a character there. But here, our opponents probably wouldn't care if they hurt a little kid.

We won. I wasn't even disappointed that I didn't get to play. I felt as though I had been part of something special. We returned to Pinyudo as heroes.

∎

I never forgot that I was at Pinyudo for a very serious purpose: to be trained to be a soldier. Over the years, boys were regularly sent away to be trained and then returned to camp. Some of them disappeared again, sent to the front line. They didn't come back.

We knew the time would come for all of us. My involvement in soccer gave me extra protection, but a couple of years after I arrived at Pinyudo, my time came, too. I was about eleven years old.

Occasionally, news got back to us about our friends who had been chosen to go to war and hadn't made it. It didn't put me off. It fed my desire for revenge, and the hatred in my heart.

It has been widely reported that both the government of Sudan and the Sudan People's Liberation Army recruited children and trained them to be soldiers during the civil war—although they have each denied arming minors.

It is believed that Sudanese child soldiers numbered in the thousands. Many of them were armed and sent to the front line, where they became killers and were killed.

Some of the children joined voluntarily, perhaps out of a desire to avenge the deaths of their families. But there are also reports of some unaccompanied children being abducted and forced to take up arms.

International charities and aid organisations remain concerned that the practice of recruiting child soldiers continues in some countries.

6

Soldier School

I knew what to do with a gun. I knew how to hold it. I knew how to fire at the enemy. I wasn't afraid to kill.

I knew all of this before I had even started my training with the army.

I was comfortable around guns. It wasn't hard to find an AK-47 at Pinyudo camp. Some of the army men carried them around and they'd let us play with them. Most of the time, they were loaded. Guns were like toys to us. We'd cock our guns, and pretend we were shooting each other. I recognised that there was a great irony to this— we were making fun with guns, the weapons that were used to kill our people throughout southern Sudan. But playing with a gun made me feel empowered. When I held a gun, I felt no fear. I thought owning a gun would make me a man. It would make me a soldier.

There were unfortunate accidents, though. Occasionally a boy picked up a gun not knowing it was loaded, pulled the trigger and accidentally shot himself.

The army men sporadically selected boys for training during morning parade. The boys who had gone before us would return to camp, bragging about their experiences, and make fun of those of us who were uninitiated.

One morning, I was chosen. They told me to pack my things and be ready to go that night.

The SPLA was providing military training to children. They must have known the global outrage this simple fact would cause, because they were secretive about it. They didn't want the aid workers to know. By day, Pinyudo had the appearance of a refugee camp. By night, the army came in.

But I wanted this. So when I was chosen, I didn't protest. I willingly joined the other boys for the walk that would take several hours and finally make me a soldier.

The training would go on for a few weeks. Because there were so many boys, we were divided into two batches. I wanted to be in the first group, and I was. I packed a bag with a pair of shorts, a blanket and a sheet to sleep on, and I carefully carried my socker ball in my hands.

We had been walking for a few hours when men emerged from nowhere and began beating us with sticks. They seemed to jump out of the trees, beating us and screaming, 'You stupid recruits!'

We fled. I ran hard, but not fast enough. I dropped my bag as a man whacked me hard across the back with a stick. I fell heavily, flat on my stomach, somehow still clinging to my socker ball.

'Get up!' the man screamed, not pausing in beating me. 'If you're going to be a soldier, you have to be tough!'

My physical pain was mingled with exhilaration. I wanted this to happen. I couldn't be a soldier without going through this. I had been psychologically prepared. The boys who had been trained before us had warned us this would happen.

I clung to my socker ball. I had lost my bag while running away but I didn't care. As long as I had my ball.

The men who had beaten us were the trainers. Before we had time to recover, a serious-looking man ordered us to stand to attention. I held onto my ball, and listened carefully to his words. We had only just arrived and, without wanting to, I had already caught his attention. 'What's your name?' he demanded.

I told him, and was immediately ridiculed. 'Look at this idiot. What does he think this is—a place of play?' he said. The other boys laughed. I was the only kid dumb enough to bring a ball to training. What was I thinking? Soldiers don't carry balls, especially not balls made out of a sock. They carry guns.

'We're not here to play, you stupid,' he continued. 'How could you come here with a ball? You're not a man. Do you think this is a playground? This is a battlefield!'

I stood there, scared and ashamed, and copped it. He took out his gun and began shooting the dirt around me. I forced myself to stand to attention, unmoving, even though I wanted to jump and run. 'Let me tell you what this place is,' he said as he continued making a circle of gunshots around my quivering body. 'You're here to be a soldier!'

Two more men came after me with sticks and I ran, as they chased me into the river. I jumped into the water and stayed in there until they ordered me to get out. They forced me to roll around on the ground, dripping wet, coating my body in mud. There was no point arguing with them. They wouldn't have understood what my socker ball represented.

I didn't care where I slept. I had grown used to sleeping rough. But I couldn't bear to be separated from my ball. Soccer to me was everything. But they confiscated my socker ball, and burnt it. As I watched the flames destroy it, the anger flared inside me. I refused to let them see it.

It seemed to be their preferred way of taking treasured things from us. Like the rosary beads given to us by the nuns. Many of us wore the beads around our necks, until a trainer yanked them from our necks, threw them in a pile on the ground and set them alight, while shouting: 'Do you think this is a place of worship?'

We said nothing. But afterwards, amongst ourselves, we quietly wondered why he did it.

■

We hadn't eaten for hours, and I was starving. 'There's no food here,' one of the men told us. 'Did you guys bring food?'

We shook our heads. 'All right,' he said. 'If you don't want food, it's up to you.'

They told us to find a place to sleep. We had walked for hours to get here, but we wouldn't eat tonight. I lay in the dirt and tried to fall asleep, only to be abruptly woken half an hour later by a piercing whistle.

'You stupids, you think this is a fucking holiday? Get up!' the men shouted, taking out their big sticks and beating us again.

'Stand to attention and don't move,' they shouted as we scrambled to obey. 'Even if a fly touches your face, don't move an inch!'

I couldn't help but feel exhilarated again. It was tough love, and I wanted it. I felt like I had been working towards this moment since the day I had left Wau.

They made us stand there for hours, in the middle of the night, just standing there unmoving. Standing straight and doing nothing is harder than it sounds. Some of the boys were so tired that they fell over.

'OK, you can go to sleep now,' the men said. We crashed wherever we could, only to be woken again half an hour later by the screeching whistle. 'Time to get up, you stupid recruits!' they bellowed.

It wasn't even sunrise, and we had not slept or eaten. For some boys, it was already too much; they had tried to sneak out. But they were caught, brought back and beaten.

■

The training started with simple things, like 'at ease', 'attention', words that you associate with being a soldier. That was the fun bit. And of course they gave us food, which they made us cook ourselves—how else would we have survived the training?

I looked for ways to distinguish myself. I could already handle an AK-47 with skill. I was less enthusiastic when they made us crawl in the mud. Sometimes they threw in faeces and made us crawl through the slippery mix in the rain. We reeked of poo.

The worst part for me was crawling uphill through the mud. My knees and elbows were bleeding and my arms were blistered, as I slid and slipped through the stinking mud. They made us carry a stick in

This hut in the village of Wau is typical of what people in South Sudan live in today, often with many other people, and is similar to the hut I lived in with my parents as a young child.

This is the special photo of Emmanuel and me that I carried from Ethiopia to Kenya and Australia. It was taken during one of the interviews we did with the white people in Ethiopia. I didn't know who they were, but Pieng was there and said it was OK for us to talk to them.

This was taken in a town called Eldoret in Kenya, during a music festival I attended when I was in the choir at the boarding school I went to. I don't know who the car belongs to. But touching it felt good.

Kakuma Refugee Camp in 2003—a sprawling township in the middle of the desert. (Image © Christophe Calais / Corbis)

This was Daudi the legend, playing for the Kakuma central camp team! When I look at this picture it reminds me of being happy all the time. I have never found that happiness again, because I worry too much about other people and my country. It was taken by Noriaki before he died. We won that day. Behind me is Taban Abraham, who now plays in my team here, the Western Tigers. Not only is he one of the most experienced players, he is also a very good friend.

Hanging out after church in the hut I shared with my friend Bank Anei. And in the middle is our friend Aring Madut.

The Black Eagles Holy Cross team in Kakuma, just before a match kick off. We had a one minute silence for Noriaki, who had just died. Most of these boys are now in the US. Taban, Nhial and Beny are in Melbourne. These boys were legends!

I didn't see much of my cousin Archangelo in Kenya because he was at a school outside the camp. In this picture, I was visiting him at his school. We were sharing a meal together before he left for Australia.

our arms that we pretended was a gun, as we crawled from side to side, looking out for the enemy.

I was struggling, and other boys overtook me with ease. 'You're letting the team down!' one of the men screamed at me. 'The enemy is catching up and you're putting everyone else at risk!'

He stood on my back, emphasising my weakness. With his full weight on my back I couldn't move at all. I was skinny for an eleven-year-old. 'I can't move,' I mumbled breathlessly as I fought back the tears and the pain.

'Look, everyone,' the man shouted, still on my back. 'The enemy has caught up with us and we're dead. And it's all because of one stupid soldier who couldn't move . . . This is a battlefield, and what you do here will serve you in the battleground. If you are stupid, you will be the first to die and you will endanger your comrades.'

His words made me feel terrible. The last thing I wanted was for my friends to die because of me. But with the burly man's full weight still on my back, I wasn't crawling anywhere.

They wouldn't tolerate weakness in a kid, and my punishment was harsh. They made me take off my clothes and stand to attention, naked beneath the blazing African sun. Then they all went off and had lunch. They idly watched me sweltering under the sun, their eating interspersed with mockery: 'Lazy, stupid recruit.'

I was humiliated. I stood there, unmoving, until I was dismissed a couple of hours later. I ran to the river and dunked my bruised body in the water. But the physical pain was superseded by the feeling that I had let my comrades down.

The nights were no easier. We took it in turns to be on night watch for two hours at a time. During the day, I learnt to memorise the shape of the trees so that when darkness came, I didn't confuse them with the enemy.

They say that soldiers don't sleep with both eyes closed. 'Don't sleep like a woman,' they told us. A soldier can be only half asleep— because to sleep deeply could mean death for all of us.

∎

The men wanted us to sing military songs. They were songs of bravery and songs of hate. One afternoon, one of the men unexpectedly announced: 'We're going to learn the next song from David.'

Oh God! I didn't know how to make up a song!

'Go, David,' he said. 'You have two hours to rest and think of a new song, and then come back and teach us.'

I don't know why he picked me. I could put a gun together, I could kick a soccer ball with skill, but I wasn't a poet! I sat on my own, my anxiety growing, my mind blank. I couldn't think of anything, let alone a good tune or line.

We had been taught to always obey orders. Even if they told you to jump into a fire, you had to do it without question. But this was something I could not do. I even thought about Mama, praying that memories of her would give me some inspiration. They didn't. My two hours were up, and I had nothing. I was damned.

The boys were all standing to attention when I emerged. 'Go on, David, teach us your song,' the trainer said. I stood there dumbly.

'Go on, I'm waiting for you,' he said. Everyone was staring at me. I knew I was in big trouble. The minutes ticked by and still, I said nothing.

'All right, people,' he said. 'You can go. You're lucky. Since David hasn't come up with a song, you can all have free time.' He paused. 'I will deal with you, David.'

I did try to protest, to tell them that not everyone could compose a song. 'I don't have any talent,' I yelled, scrambling to defend myself as the men grabbed me.

It was no use. They dragged me across the ground, kicked me, tied my feet together, threw my body into the water until I was sure I was going to drown, and then pulled me out as I choked and gasped.

I endured every punishment the trainers chose to dish out, and I bore them no ill will. I reasoned that it was a necessary part of my training. I needed this to be a soldier and to join my brothers on Sudan's front line.

I felt like I'd screwed up again. I wanted to do something to prove myself. I got my chance. During one exercise, we had to camouflage ourselves. They told us to be creative, to think about how we'd hide on the battlefield so we didn't end up dead.

They gave us time to prepare. Lots of the boys went for the obvious idea of cutting down tree branches and tying them around themselves. But I wanted to do something different. I knew I had to take a risk if I was to stand out.

I found a hill very close to where we'd set up camp. I dug a hole in the dirt, mixed some water with soil and smeared it all over myself. Then I jumped into the hole.

It was a very obvious place to hide. So obvious that no-one thought to look there. I stayed in my hiding spot for ages. Even when most of the boys had been found, I quietly waited, smiling to myself as boys walked right past but didn't see me.

There were just a couple of us left when we finally emerged from our hiding places to cheers. Another boy had come up with a brilliant idea—he had climbed a tree, and surrounded himself with branches while keeping his balance.

I was proud to be one of the last. I felt that I had finally redeemed myself.

■

On graduation day, they called us 'soldiers' for the first time. I was no longer just a recruit. I walked with my skinny chest sticking out, feeling like a big man.

As we graduated, another group of boys were on their way to start training. And just as we had been ambushed, it was payback time.

We hid in trees, holding sticks, and jumped on the boys as they walked beneath us. We swore at them and beat them with our sticks. Even though I was beating my brothers, it felt good; it was a way of forgetting my own pain.

The trainers ordered us not to tell the white people where we had been. I felt bad that I couldn't tell the aid workers. They were there to help us, and they would have been horrified if they knew. But I didn't feel like a victim. No-one had forced me to do anything. The army made me tough and I appreciated it. If I had not acquired that toughness when I was little, I probably wouldn't be here now.

■

Soon after our return to camp, it was time to choose the next batch of boys to go to war—and in many cases, to their deaths.

I desperately wanted to go. But I knew that I was small. I needed a plan. I grabbed a blanket and a small stool. As we gathered in the assembly, I stood on the stool and wrapped myself in the blanket, so they couldn't tell that I had artificially enhanced my height. I hoped it would be enough.

Damn! The trainer who walked down our line knew me. I wouldn't be able to fool him. I knew he wouldn't risk picking me because I was too little. I begged him: 'Please, please, please, let me go. I'm good with a gun!'

'We can't risk it, David,' he said.

I felt so bitter. I had romanticised war and death in my mind. Dying for South Sudan would have been a great honour.

But much later I realised that I was very lucky. If I had been picked, I'd probably be dead. Like my cousin Bol. He was a few years older than me, a proud young man. And he was chosen. He came to see me in the camp the night before he left. I begged him not to go. I didn't care about sacrificing my own life. But I didn't want that for him.

A few months later, word got back to us that he had been killed. The saddest thing is that to this day, no-one knows where his body is. His family has never had closure.

The war is littered with stories like this, of boys who were killed, their bodies left for the vultures. So many boys died and were never paid the final respect of a proper burial.

They stayed in the Ethiopian camps for more than four years. And then, in 1991, Ethiopia went through a political crisis of its own. When the Mengistu government was overthrown by Ethiopian rebels, the Sudanese refugees were forced to flee the camps that had become their homes.

Later that year, the situation in Sudan deteriorated further, with an internal split within the Sudan People's Liberation Army. Riek Machar, a Nuer who held a senior position in the army, tried and failed to topple its leader John Garang de Mabior, a Dinka. As the fighting between the north and the south continued, tribal war between the Dinkas and the Nuer was also breaking out in the south.

What followed in the town of Bor was one of Sudan's deadliest tribal massacres, where thousands of Dinkas were killed.

7

Hunted

I made a new soccer ball when we returned to camp, careful not to tell the white people our secret. I was now officially a soldier, but life had returned to being as normal as it could be.

The army was still recruiting boys for the front line. I tried very hard to persuade them to let me go. But they never picked me.

One day, our most special visitor yet was due to arrive. The excitement rippled throughout the camp as we went about cleaning, making everything perfect for him, singing military songs, our spirits high.

While most Western kids my age were idolising 1980s and 1990s pop stars, my hero was the man who had inspired the uprising against the government of Sudan—John Garang de Mabior. And he was coming to Pinyudo to talk to us.

It was a privilege for us to be addressed by our great leader. The area where we usually held parade was packed. I arrived early to get a spot near the front. I could see him up close, looking distinguished in his military khakis.

I clung to his every word. His message was very clear—that we were the next generation, the seeds of tomorrow, and all the fighting was for our sake. You have to get an education, he told us, because once South Sudan is liberated, you will be its future leaders.

He told us that the northern forces had destroyed our homes and driven us away. That's why we had to fight. He told us that we were supposed to be at home with our parents and going to school, but these basic rights had been denied us. He listed the towns the rebels had captured, and made it sound like we were winning the war.

His words were embedded in my head long after he left. The SPLA was all over the camp. But appearances by someone from the outside world were rare in Pinyudo. Our lives in the camp were carefully controlled. The only news that got back to us was of the war in Sudan and of our friends who had perished. The only reality we knew was the one in which we reluctantly lived.

So when danger loomed, many of us weren't prepared for it.

■

Unbeknown to us, trouble was unfolding in Ethiopia. Ethiopian rebels were taking up arms against the Mengistu government. While Mengistu remained in power, we could enjoy his protection. But once his government was overthrown we would be in great danger.

We had fled the war in our country, only to land right in the thick of one that was erupting in another. The Ethiopian rebels were advancing, headed for our camp, and the SPLA could not keep them at bay. It was only a matter of time before they invaded Pinyudo.

The first warning we had of imminent danger was the sudden increased presence of the army. By then, the situation had become desperate—we had to get out fast.

Men from the army told us our best bet was to walk back to southern Sudan. But I thought they were crazy. Our boys had been going back there to fight in the war, only to get killed. We had two choices: we could take on the Sudanese guns or the Ethiopian guns. Either way, we were condemned. Death now seemed inevitable to me—the only question was at whose hands would I die?

We left our escape too late. By the time we made a run for it, the gunshots were already audible in the distance.

If I was going to run for my life, at least this time I'd get to do it in shoes. I didn't fancy another long trek in blistered bare feet. I grabbed the backpack I had sewn together myself, and stuffed a sheet and blanket into it. I carefully packed the photo of me and my dear friend Emmanuel, but I didn't bother taking my soccer ball.

I didn't have time to look for Emmanuel. Nor did I look for Baba. By now, we barely saw each other. It was every man for himself.

The camp had descended into a confusion of people running wildly, searching for safety. We didn't follow the main path. We didn't want to risk our killers spotting us. We slipped into the bush and pushed our way through it. I found myself running in a small group with some other boys and a man that I didn't know. We stayed together. The gunshots were getting louder and increasing in frequency. I decided that I had no choice but to trust the stranger who by default had become our leader. 'OK, let's be quiet and run,' he told us, taking charge. 'Our goal is the river.'

We sprinted to the Gilo River, the same crocodile-infested water we had crossed to get to Pinyudo—the river that later would become notorious as a scene of mass death.

It had been calm for our first crossing by boat four years ago. But now it was badly flooded, the current surging. We looked around, faces frantic, searching for a way out before the Ethiopians got to us.

The rebels had us in their sights now. The riverbank was inundated with gunfire as they drove past us in jeeps, shooting.

It was either death by river or death by guns. Some boys were so desperate to dodge the gunfire that they jumped into the river, taking their chances with the dual terrors of the surging current and the crocodiles. Maybe they thought being roughly tossed around by the river and drowning was a more pleasant way to die. Boys who couldn't swim jumped onto the boys who could and clung to them, only for both of them to be swept away to their deaths.

The shooting from the rebels was relentless. Their plan was clear— to force us all to jump into the river or get shot. It wasn't much of a choice, was it? But with a remarkable calm, the stranger who was our leader urged us to stay put, thinking fast.

We were near a place that the SPLA used to bring guns into Ethiopia. It was kind of like a port where they stored guns. As we watched boys get killed, we had a choice—run for our lives or pick up a gun and fight.

It seemed that the latter option was our best chance. The Ethiopians were blocking our only means of escape. They had us all trapped, and there was little time to formulate a plan. The stranger ran to the place with the guns and we followed. 'All of you grab a gun and fire at the same time in the same direction,' he said urgently. 'We need to create an opening to get past them.'

We each grabbed a gun and together we returned fire. We had to get past six or seven men shooting at us. But we had the numbers—there were more than ten of us. Together, we turned our guns on the men, quickly moving towards them at the same time.

It was a good strategy. They retreated as we advanced, firing our guns. I don't know if I killed anyone. I wouldn't have cared if I had. We persisted in shooting until we had forced them to move back enough to create a small opening, enough for us to run past them.

I concentrated on running, running past the rebels, running along the riverbank, running until we came across a more placid section of the river. We jumped in and swam and swam and swam, the adrenaline and fear giving us the broad shoulders of Olympic swimmers.

We emerged from the water when we thought we were safe and headed for the riverbank. There were other survivors already there. Together, we half-walked, half-ran, back to Pochalla. Back to southern Sudan.

I wasn't panting from all the running. Soccer had made me fit. Still, instead of celebrating my survival, I felt depleted. I couldn't stop thinking about the desperate scene at the river. More dead people. I was so tired of watching people die.

Now that we had escaped Ethiopia, I had time to dwell on the terror of being back in Sudan. I felt like there was a death sentence over my head, and I was simply waiting for the day I would be hanged. I had no concept of a future.

More and more survivors were arriving after us in Pochalla. I looked around frantically for Emmanuel, but I couldn't find him.

I walked through the crowd of thousands, asking people I knew if they had seen him. Nobody had. I made the bleak assumption that he must be dead.

But Lueth was there. And I found my father. He had crossed the river with some of the others. We were happy to see each other, but there was no visible emotion. There were no hugs. That's just how it was between us.

■

We had to start from scratch in Pochalla, building our own huts again. It was a small township, dusty and remote. Our only food was whatever animals we could hunt and kill. We foraged for food as the weeks went by and we slowly starved. I was sure this was it now. I had already defied death many times before. Surely I couldn't get away with it for much longer.

One day I heard a plane in the distance. I looked up and watched it approach. Then it seemed to pause over our heads. Maybe the white people had come to help us? The fleeting thought quickly vanished and I watched in horror as the bombs began to fall out of the sky.

There were terrified screams as people dropped to the ground. The arseholes had the advantage of surprise. We weren't expecting the airstrikes, and we had done nothing to prepare ourselves. So many people died that first time. We buried their bodies—dutifully and devoid of emotion.

We dug massive trenches to protect ourselves. We covered them with trees and leaves and soil, leaving just a small opening for us to cram into. I wondered if I was digging my own grave. My greatest fear was that a bomb would land directly in the hole that was meant to be our sanctuary, and we'd be buried alive. It was too horrible to contemplate—being cramped in a dark place, unable to escape, utterly conscious of your fate as you died a slow death. We had to take the risk, though. And in the end, I think it saved lives.

Each time we heard the familiar hum of a plane in the distance, we crammed into our trenches in the dirt. If you happened to be too far away, you'd immediately fall flat, stomach pressed to the dirt, head down.

Even if the bombs didn't find you, there was no shortage of ways to die. We were eating less and less. My faith in God—the faith that I had depended on to get me through Ethiopia—was faltering. I watched people, faces and bodies beyond gaunt, literally starve to death.

We were forced to find creative ways to feel full. One boy managed to find some tobacco, and we each took it in turns to smoke it. Apparently, smoking the tobacco made you thirstier, and we'd drink more water from the river. Perhaps by filling our bellies with water, we reasoned, we could trick our minds into thinking we were full. It actually worked.

I didn't sleep, remembering what I had been taught during my soldier training. To sleep was to die. We could only ever be half-asleep. Each night we packed what few belongings we had, so that there'd be no delay if we came under fire and had to run.

One day I went hunting with a man named Ayom, hoping we'd stumble across something to eat. It wasn't looking good. We paused beneath a tree. I looked up and saw something move.

'Look! There's a monkey!' I cried.

'There's no way we can eat it,' Ayom said. 'Monkeys are like human beings.'

'But we're starving!' I argued.

We bickered about it for some time. 'Fine,' I said. 'If you don't want to shoot it, I will.'

And before he could say another word, I cocked my gun, aimed and fired. Man, I was good! I could hear the cry of the monkey as it fell from the tree. But I didn't care.

Ayom was totally grossed out. 'I'm not touching it,' he declared, marching back to camp. The dead monkey and I were alone together. I couldn't wait to eat it.

By the time I got back to camp, the others had been warned. They were starving—but they weren't going to eat a monkey.

One by one, I cut off each limb and the tail and thoroughly cleaned the insides. I paused to admire my work. Once I'd severed the head you couldn't even tell it was a monkey. I started a fire, grabbed the pot and filled it with water. I added the chopped monkey to the boiling water. We didn't have any onions or herbs, but we did have salt. I seasoned the pieces of boiling monkey with salt, and let it cook well.

It smelled good! So good that the aroma brought some of the others over to come and see it. 'Hey, everyone, who wants some food?' I said. I helped myself to a serve of salted monkey, sat beneath a tree and took a bite. It was really tasty, kind of like beef. I fell asleep, satisfied. Clearly I wasn't the only one—when I woke, there was no monkey left.

■

Life continued in this way—a desperate scramble for food, diving into our trenches, and burying the bodies of our friends.

But then a rare morale booster arrived in the form of Manute Bol, a Sudanese basketballer who had made it big in America. He went to a great deal of trouble to visit us, travelling for hours through Kenya to get to Pochalla. And he cried when he saw us.

At the same time, the journalists started coming. Their graphic words and pictures put pressure on the government of Sudan and horrified the world. For the first time since we had fled Ethiopia, the planes that flew over our heads would be from the United Nations. And they'd drop food instead of bombs.

The thought of food gave our diminished bodies the strength to cut down trees and clear the bush so the pilots would know where to drop the food.

We heard the plane, as always, before we saw it. By now, we had mastered its sound. We were wary though—we didn't know if we should run for our holes in the ground or stick around to see if it was the food we had been told was coming. We stood our ground as large white sacks fell out of the sky.

There were cries as we all rushed forward at once. So many sacks! Some people stupidly tried to catch the heavy sacks of maize and sorghum and were crushed beneath them. We dragged the sacks to our camp. I was so hungry that I didn't wait to cook the food. I ate handfuls of sorghum raw while waiting for the rest to boil. It was hard, but OK to swallow if you chewed it for a while.

I don't know what happened, but before long the food stopped. And the bombardment from the sky resumed.

■

One day, Baba came and found me. 'David, it's too dangerous to stay here,' he said. 'We have to leave again.'

So we walked again, to a place called Pakok. The refugees from the Dimma camp were already there. They had gone there directly from Ethiopia. The plan now was for the rest of us from the Pinyudo and Itang camps to join them. There were thousands of us, although our numbers had fallen drastically since we'd first gone to Ethiopia four or five years earlier. Death had taken so many of our friends.

Baba did some work for a woman from the Red Cross in Pakok. In return, she told him that she would let Baba and me go with her in the Red Cross truck further south to another town, Kapoeta. It was a bigger place, and she said we'd be safer there. We were very grateful for her kindness.

Kapoeta was a large town, and the SPLA presence was strong. We stayed with a relative in an overcrowded hut with more than twenty other people. It was too packed for us to all sleep inside, so the men slept outside. I would have been about thirteen years old, and I considered myself a man. I had made a blanket and a sheet to sleep on by sewing together some old sorghum sacks.

We stayed in Kapoeta for a few months. But the planes eventually followed us. We dug more holes to hide from the bombs, wearily resigned to the fact that the northern forces were determined to kill us. Then Baba found me and told me we had to leave again.

We continued our trek south until we got to the town of Narus. Since fleeing Ethiopia, we had gradually been inching south towards the Kenyan border. We were so close to Kenya that the aid workers could more easily get to us now.

But our enemies from the north got to us, too—picking up where they left off with their bombardment from the sky.

The refugees continued to flee south. When the Sudanese government's forces captured Kapoeta—a town that had previously been held by the Sudan People's Liberation Army— their journey became all the more desperate.

As they walked, they were chased by air and land attacks. Many died along the way, killed in airstrikes or by starvation.

In 1992 the refugees crossed another border. This time, they shifted their hopes to a refugee camp in Kenya in the town of Kakuma. According to UNICEF, at least 20 000 of the refugees were unaccompanied minors, mainly from the Dinka and Nuer tribes. The aid workers began to call them the Lost Boys.

8

Minors

The moment I physically parted with Sudan, I sensed that I had made my last long walk. I never wanted to go back to Sudan. I now considered myself a stateless person.

My faith was still wavering. If there was a God, then where was He? Why was He letting so many people starve? I used to pray each night and each morning. But I felt that God was ignoring me.

Entering Kenya meant bidding farewell to the Sudan People's Liberation Army. The Kenyans would accept only refugees. There would be no children with guns here.

Since we had fled the Gilo River in Ethiopia, I had carried the gun that had helped me escape. The gun was nestled in a corner of my bag.

A Kenyan policeman rummaged through my bag and found my gun. 'Why do you have this?' he barked, taking my AK-47. 'Here in Kenya you can't carry a gun.'

To him, I was just a teenage refugee. He probably didn't know that I owed my life to that gun, that I had trained to be a soldier, that I could identify the gun that was strapped to him without even touching it. For a child, my expertise on guns was scary.

I had a connection to the weapon, and once you have that connection it takes you to another world. By giving the Kenyan man my gun, I was saying 'bye bye' to that world. It was 1992, I was fourteen years old, and the war in Sudan had been raging for almost a decade. It was time to move into a new world.

■

Lokichogio is a giant dusty abyss in Kenya near the Sudanese border. We marched across the border and into our new country.

I couldn't believe how hot and windy it was. The dust storms would come and the sand would sting your eyes. When you had food in your hands, you had to gulp it down quickly. If you paused while your food travelled the short distance to your mouth you'd end up eating dust.

The aid workers gave us the materials to build our huts and set up camp. We had only just arrived but already I could see a clear difference—you couldn't just randomly cut down trees here. This was Kenya, a country with laws. Cutting down trees or killing animals for food could get you into serious trouble.

Those that did the wrong thing faced the hostility of the local tribe, the Turkana people. It was little wonder they didn't like us. You wouldn't want a bunch of strangers turning up at your house, unannounced, and competing for the same scarce resources.

I hadn't felt so uncomfortably hot since our Sahara trek. It was routinely forty degrees Celsius. At least here there was the odd tree. During the hottest part of the day, the heat was so intense that it totally sapped my energy. All I could do was lie under a tree all day. It was boring. Still, I preferred being bored to being bombed.

It's less than fifty kilometres from Lokichogio to the Sudanese border—too close to feel safe.

The United Nations wanted to move us deeper into Kenya. Our time in Lokichogio would be mercifully brief. One morning, the aid workers told us to pack our modest possessions and get ready. We were moving some ninety kilometres away to Kakuma, with the blessing of the Kenyan president, Daniel arap Moi.

My instincts had been correct—there'd be no more walking in the blistering heat. We would travel in big Red Cross trucks.

The whole operation was so well organised, moving us group by group in the big trucks, that I began fantasising about what Kakuma would be like. I imagined we'd have proper houses, and they'd be ready for us. We wouldn't have to build a thing.

Baba and I pulled ourselves up onto the back of a truck and stood with dozens of others for the dusty drive to Kakuma. I barely glimpsed a tree or anything green on the way.

There were tens of thousands of people from the three Ethiopian camps. We'd all be together at the same camp now.

Our truck came to a halt and with it, my illusions of our new home. I glanced around at the vast, empty space. Were they kidding? I had grown used to living in harsh conditions. Pinyudo may have been horrible, but at least it had trees and a rainy season. Did these people actually expect us to live in the desert?

Despite my trepidation, I resolved to accept this place would be my home for a long time. There was nowhere else to go.

∎

It was far from heaven and there was a serious shortage of food, but Kakuma was the closest thing to normal life that I had ever experienced. While Pinyudo camp had been controlled by the army, there was none of that here. We still couldn't wander around as we wished; it felt more like a prison with freedom than a military camp.

There was no assembly in the morning, no beatings, no talk of war, no Poo Police. We were no longer '*jaysh ahmar*', 'red army'. They called us 'minors'. We were finally being recognised as children who had gone through something terrible.

I was beginning to feel quite human. I felt that something good could happen. There might still be days when I didn't have food. But that was OK. I'd have food tomorrow.

The mood in the camp was lighter, too. We were protected from news from the outside. There was no more news from the front line of our friends who had gone to war and been killed.

My connection with Sudan was less and less. I had a glimpse from the local Kenyans of how life could be—with a mother, a father, and children. A stable family in a stable house that wasn't in danger of being burnt to the ground. I felt hope.

We had to start from scratch again. I hoped this would be the last time. Building a hut had become quite tedious, but I had become an expert. I was quite skilled at layering the twigs and poking the mud mixed with water into the holes to make the walls, smoothing them down with my hands. The roof was a plastic sheet, which was completely useless in this heat. I pinned my cherished photo of Emmanuel and me to the wall inside my hut, using a thorn to lodge the photo into the mud-brick wall.

Imagine that your bed each night sits inside an oven, and the oven is switched on high. That's how hot it felt inside the hut. I lay outside most of the time, using the hut mainly to store what few belongings I had and for a (rare) rainy day. At least I had a place to call home.

It hardly mattered, because sleep continued to evade me anyway. I couldn't shrug off the fear that we'd be raided again, just as we had been in Pinyudo. I had thought that we would be safe there, too. I braced myself for the enemy to invade our new camp and try to kill us as we slept.

■

That first year in Kakuma was tough. Water was seriously scarce. Even with the water tanks, there was barely enough for drinking, let alone bathing and washing clothes.

We started a new school beneath a tree and finally had something to do to fill the days and escape the intensity of the sun. The shade was our classroom; my finger was my pen; the dirt on the ground in front of me was my notebook. This made it impossible to take our notes away with us, so we crammed everything we had learnt that day into our heads.

When I look back, it seems like a strange way to learn, but at the time I had nothing to compare it to. I had longed for an education and, at least for now, this was the closest I would get.

I also became reacquainted with my other love—soccer. I asked around the camp for a sock and made a new socker ball. Late in the day, when the sun dipped, we played for hours. I would have played all day if it wasn't so hot. Sometimes, we'd settle for juggling the ball beneath a tree as we waited for the air to cool slightly.

Life was very simple. But with soccer and our lessons beneath the tree, I was content. At least there were no more bombs dropping out of the sky.

The camp was plagued with disease, although the hygiene conditions were far superior to what they had been in Pinyudo. At least we had clean water. Initially there was just one medical clinic. You wouldn't want to get sick. The queues were so ridiculous that you could die before you saw someone. A friend of ours became very sick with malaria. We joined the back of the long line at the clinic. 'Hey man,' I told him. 'You'd better pretend that you're in pain and dying. Otherwise you'll be here all night!'

On cue, he fainted and lay there on the ground, spluttering and pretending to die a slow death. 'Oh my God, he's dying!' we shouted.

A nurse rushed out and we carried him to the front of the queue. He actually was very sick. Malaria is a very serious business. By African standards, though, he wasn't sick enough.

There were plenty of ways to die in Kakuma. Disease swept through the camp. People hooked up in the camp and got married and had children. It was a terrible place to have babies. Infants were born to parents who could barely feed themselves, and their babies were seriously malnourished.

There was a food distribution centre inside the camp, but we had to carefully manage our food ration to make it last for two weeks. One ration of food might be a cup of oil and some maize and beans. Sometimes we'd get self-raising flour and lentils. It was never enough to last the fortnight. We tried to make do by pooling our resources. We'd combine the rations of ten people so they'd go further. But even then, our joint resources were only enough to make one modest meal a day for each of us.

We were quite smart about economising, and nothing was wasted. But our rations always ran out before the two weeks did, and we'd have a couple of days when we had to go without food entirely. They gave us food to sustain us, not to satisfy us. But we were used to it—that was life, and you didn't complain.

Meat was gold, and I craved it. If I'd wanted meat in Sudan, I killed an animal. But you couldn't do that in Kenya. In Ethiopia, we didn't care about pissing off the locals because we had guns. We didn't care what they would do. But here in Kenya, without our guns, we were less brave.

Still, the locals often blamed us if an animal died overnight beside one of our huts—even if it wasn't our fault. If you discovered a dead animal near your hut, you'd drag it as far away as you could just to avoid an argument.

It took a long time, but the tension between the locals and us eventually eased. I think it all began with the water. As more water tanks were brought in, there was enough water to share with the locals. They'd enter the camp and bring their animals to drink our water. I think it dawned on them that having the refugees around came with benefits for them, too.

Things began to settle down soon after that. Relations became civil, and then almost friendly. We began bartering food. We'd give them some of our sorghum and maize and beans and sometimes, when they slaughtered an animal, they would let us have some meat.

The locals sometimes used our camp as a shortcut to get from one end of the village to the other. We even picked up some of their language, Swahili. '*Hakuna matata*!'—'No worries!'—they'd say after a disagreement had been resolved.

We began to see more of the Kenyans when our camp got its first real school. We were given the materials to build our own schools, in the same way we had built our huts. Some of the locals were too poor to send their children to the schools in Kakuma town, so they used ours.

At last, at the age of about fourteen or fifteen, I sat in a classroom for the first time and began to get the education that I had craved.

Young teachers arrived from Kenya. I saw my first real blackboard and chalk, and then the exercise books and pencils came. No more writing with my finger in the dirt.

When the textbooks arrived, I was keen to do as much reading as I could. The standard of my reading and writing improved dramatically. My goal was to read so well that I could read the Bible from cover to cover. As life had slowly improved in the camp, I had made my peace with God and returned to my faith. Once I gained more confidence with my English, I asked Abuna Madol, who had made the trek to Kenya with us, if I could borrow a copy of the Bible. I told him I wanted to know the whole story.

Through the Don Bosco organisation we were given the opportunity to learn practical skills such as carpentry, electrical wiring, masonry and plumbing. It was as though we were being prepared for life outside of the camp—although there was nowhere for us to apply our new skills. Where on earth would we go?

It had taken a long time to get these opportunities, and I took them very seriously. Education was the main game for me and many of my friends. It was like we had joined all the dots in our lives, and connected them to the speech that John Garang de Mabior had made in Pinyudo. He had implored the young boys of southern Sudan to get an education. And we were responding.

We competed with each other, but we also helped each other. Test results were publicly displayed and we were ranked from first to last. You would be shamed or respected depending on your result.

My friends and I formed a study group. It was an exclusive club. One of the boys in the group was my friend Dominic, who had survived the airstrikes and made the trek to Kenya with me. Each person in the group had to add value in some way, to help the other boys. We sat beneath a tree and tested ourselves and each other.

There was one guy at school who always struggled. I found myself wanting to help him and invited him to join our study group. The other boys weren't happy with me. They said this guy couldn't bring anything to the group. But I persisted. I told them that he might not bring anything to the group, but he could learn from us. I got my way and he joined our group. With our help, he moved up the ranking in the class. I felt really good about that.

There were about seventy kids in our class—and just one girl. I don't know how that happened. There were many more boys than girls in the camp. Naturally, some of the other guys began hitting on her.

Boys going through puberty can be immature little shits and it must have been tough for her. Especially when we began learning about *that* stuff. The first time we heard the word 'menstruation', we thought it was hilarious. Maybe the poor girl thought we were using our newfound knowledge to imagine what she looked like naked. She was so uncomfortable that she stood up and stormed out.

She came back the following day, though, and I had a new respect for her. I was impressed by her courage.

■

Since we had built a church in the same way we had built our schools and huts, Sunday had become my favourite day.

Church in Kakuma wasn't a drag the way it had been when I was a kid in Wau. I was an altar boy and part of the choir. There was euphoric singing, and it went on for hours.

We looked forward to Christmas. If we were able to get paint or charcoal, we'd decorate our huts by drawing patterns on the mud walls, both inside and out. I wasn't very good at drawing so I stuck to basic flowers and horizontal stripes. Our huts looked beautiful, and it made Christmas special.

We may have been poor refugees, but we knew how to celebrate what we did have: each other. On Christmas Eve, we went to church. Dressed in whatever white clothes we could find, we'd dance around the camp while beating drums. Our procession would go out onto the streets and someone would carry a cross as we danced around the neighbourhood, singing songs. When Christmas came, we could pretend we were normal kids who hadn't missed out on anything.

On Christmas Day, we'd go to church again and spend the day visiting our friends. We saved up our food rations in the days leading up to Christmas so we could have more on the day. It might have meant less food or no food for a few days. But it was worth it to be able to cook and share our food with each other on Christmas Day.

∎

Soccer became a serious competition in Kakuma. There were a few teams, mostly divided on tribal lines. For a while we played with socker balls. And then the real soccer balls arrived.

I was old enough to play in a real team with some other boys involved in the church. We called ourselves Black Eagles Holy Cross. Eventually, boys who weren't involved in the church were allowed to join our team. Lueth, who had managed to get a security job at the camp, was involved in our team and was also a referee. He was now a young man, and got married and had a baby in Kakuma.

I feel that soccer brought us all together. Hundreds, even thousands of people from inside the camp and from Kakuma town would watch our games. Our team was really good, and we always drew a crowd.

We had a brilliant coach, William Machok. Since Emmanuel had gone, he had become my best friend. We slept in the same hut. Just as I had been a natural leader when I was little, I was now—I was chosen to be the team captain.

We had never watched a real soccer game. We were guided by our imaginations and our instincts. We had a pitch that we made ourselves by cutting down then uprooting the trees (with the permission of the locals) and levelling the ground with our hands. There was no fence around the pitch, so the crowd stood around it in a large square. The older people brought stools so they could sit in the front. Little kids climbed trees so they could see. When a player scored, the excited crowd ran onto the pitch. It would take five minutes, sometimes ten, to clear the pitch and resume the game.

For the first time we played in real soccer boots, and we had a white uniform that quickly got grubby as we slid around in the dirt.

It was through soccer that I earned a new name. I don't know who started it, but during a game the crowd began chanting 'DA-U-DI!!!' So I became Daudi, the Swahili word for 'David', and the name stuck.

I played in the midfield and my smooth skills made me very popular. But one day I couldn't play. A guy had knocked my ankle in the previous game. It was really swollen, and I'd be useless if I played. I knew I had to sit the game out and give my ankle time to heal.

When the crowd began turning up, some of the fans noticed I wasn't wearing my uniform. I was standing with the coach, helping him to get the team organised, when a couple of fans approached. 'Why isn't Daudi playing?' they demanded.

I tried to explain that I was injured. But they weren't placated, and were getting quite aggressive. I stood my ground. I told them there was no point playing if my ankle wasn't right. Besides, it wasn't as though I was the most important guy in the team. I wasn't a striker. But I was the captain.

We were down two–nil. I stood watching from the sidelines, knowing my boys were about to cop a thrashing. The fans made their displeasure known; more and more people were coming over to the coach and demanding that I play. 'You're still standing,' they said. 'Just get on the pitch.'

I could tell my team's morale was down, but what could I do? 'It's up to you, David,' the coach said. 'Just don't go too hard.'

I changed into my uniform and limped onto the pitch. It's every little boy's fantasy to be the hero, the guy who kicks the winning goal. I'd like to say that's what happened. But it didn't. I came onto the pitch, touched the ball very gingerly and didn't really do anything. We still managed to win, though. On penalties. Maybe the presence of the captain was enough to lift the team—even a captain with a stuffed ankle.

It was the first time I'd had a taste of what I could do, simply by being a good leader. I've always been a natural leader, since my days climbing poles in Wau. I have thought a lot about it and I don't know why. Maybe it's because of the way I've always related to my friends and valued and cared about them. They have always trusted me enough to put me in leadership positions. If I could lift my team's morale just by being there, I wondered, what else could I do?

■

For those first couple of years in Kakuma, we were oblivious to what was going on in Sudan. Then a new hospital opened in Lokichogio. The Sudanese wounded in the war were brought across the Kenyan border and treated at the hospital, then sent to Kakuma refugee camp. They brought news of the war with them. It effectively smashed our cocoon.

Suddenly, we were reconnected to news from home. The hate that we had been taught to carry as children was reignited as we were told more stories of the injustices done to our people. Stories of entire villages being burnt to the ground by the forces from northern Sudan, and people and animals ruthlessly slaughtered. There were stories of our people being captured and forced into slavery, of children kidnapped, given Muslim names and sent to work. They drummed into our heads the fact that we wouldn't be here, suffering and starving and away from our parents and homes, if it weren't for the northern Sudanese. With each story, the hate that I had tried to forget swelled inside my heart until I couldn't bear it.

Back in southern Sudan, they were rapidly losing men and boys. Since the internal split in the SPLA between the Dinkas and the Nuer, the SPLA had been trying to regain its strength. It needed more boys. And now it was eyeing Kakuma camp for a recruiting drive.

Men from the army came to the camp, discreetly took us boys aside and told us that things in southern Sudan were really bad. They needed our help. They'd give us a date and time where the trucks would be waiting in the darkness to take us back to southern Sudan, so we could join the fight.

I carefully thought about it, and found myself actually wanting to go. Many of my friends wanted to, too.

I think what saved me was soccer and a girl. I was running late to the place we were supposed to meet because of both those things.

By the time I got there, the trucks transporting the boys to war had gone.

At first, I thought it was a missed opportunity. But I regretted it only briefly. A couple of months later, we received news that my friend Wol, a very good soccer player, had been killed. Wol wasn't in my team, but we had been friendly rivals. And just like that he was gone.

Lots of the *jaysh ahmar* went back, and lots of them died. I considered myself lucky—I had escaped death again.

■

I was increasingly thinking about Mama and my sisters. I hadn't seen them in years. Not knowing what had happened to them was really bothering me. When one of the charities began trying to trace the lost family members of refugees, I was keen.

It was a tricky thing, because we hadn't seen our families for so long. I didn't know where to start to try to find my mother. I had left her as an eight-year-old child.

The way it worked was you'd write a letter in English and give it to one of the aid workers. You told the worker all the details you could remember about when and where you last saw your parents. A worker would try to find them, based on what little information they had been given. If a family member was found, the worker would read out the letter in English and someone would translate it, and send word back. It was a very primitive system, but it actually worked for some people, and there were families that were reunited.

We never talked about missing our families. We were matter-of-fact about our forced separation. We had accepted that there was a strong possibility our families were dead.

I wrote several letters to Mama in Wau and Abuk in Turalei. I never got a response. I prepared myself to learn that they were dead. I just wanted to know now; I longed for closure.

Some people chose to take matters into their own hands by making the long and dangerous journey back to southern Sudan. That journey seemed ridiculous to me now. What was the point of walking for several months to a destination where people were still trying to kill each other? Still, they tried to go back to their villages and their homes, or what was left of them. I don't know if they made it.

My father decided to make the same journey. Baba had held an important position in the camp. He was in charge of something like a kindergarten, looking after the younger kids. One day, he came looking for me and surprised me by saying: 'I'm going back to southern Sudan to try and find your Mama.'

'OK, that's fine,' I replied. There was no tearful goodbye. I didn't offer to go with him. I didn't want to go back. Here in Kenya, there was food, school, and soccer. Compared to Sudan, this was paradise.

■

The popularity of soccer had grown to the point where there was a central team in the camp with the most skilled players. That team was given the opportunity to play in a bigger Kenyan competition. My popularity in the camp had grown, too, and the boys chose me as their captain.

We travelled throughout Kenya to play other teams from other schools. I still loved playing in the midfield, and I shone with my skills. After one game, a Kenyan man approached me, shook my hand and said, 'I want you to play for my school.'

'How would that work?' I asked.

'You will go to the school for free if you play for us.'

Soccer and a real school—the opportunity seemed amazing. 'Yeah,' I said.

So I left my friends and moved to the school. It was like a boarding school, with dorms and bunk beds. Real beds! Years of sleeping on the hard ground made the softness of the mattress uncomfortable. It took a while for the bed to grow on me.

There was more food here, too. They provided three meals a day, but I still couldn't bring myself to eat breakfast. I had never had breakfast in my life. Each morning I'd go straight to class and wait for the other kids to finish their breakfast and join me.

Some of the kids went to great lengths to point out that I wasn't one of them. 'Refugee!' some of them mocked. I wasn't fazed. They weren't saying anything I didn't already know. I *was* a refugee!

Inside class was a struggle, too. The other kids were far ahead of me. The classes were in English, but there was also a Swahili class. Being unable to speak Swahili made it hard to make friends.

It was a miserable first week, but I didn't let it get me down. I knew my strength and how I could draw people closer to me. And that was through soccer.

The teachers must have known I had been sent to the school to play soccer. Once the kids saw me play, they must have realised it, too. Suddenly, lots of kids wanted to be my friend. I had grown used to people liking me because of what I could do with a soccer ball.

There was this guy at school. He came from money, and he thought he was a dude. He was going out with the hottest chick at school. Then the chick got a crush on me.

The Dude didn't play soccer, but he had two things that I had never had—status and money. Both those things were a big deal in Africa, and they made him popular.

I swear I didn't do anything to encourage her, but his chick started hanging around me. The first time, I was sitting at my desk and I couldn't help but notice her prettiness when she leaned over me. 'Hey, how are you doing? It's break time!' she said, holding up biscuits.

'OK,' I said, following her outside and onto the verandah. I didn't think anything of it. She was hot. Surely she wouldn't see anything in a poor refugee like me.

We talked about our classes and the camp. Then she brought up a touchy subject. 'Where are your parents?' she asked curiously. I quickly brushed her question aside. I didn't want to talk about it. I didn't want her to feel sorry for me.

'Can I come and visit the camp?' she asked.

'Sure, you can visit,' I said.

Later, she found me again at lunchtime, while I was lining up for food. 'Do you mind if I stand beside you?' she asked.

'OK,' I mumbled. We chatted randomly, but I was getting nervous. I could see that The Dude was getting agitated. Clearly, he didn't like his girl talking to me.

He marched over and interrupted our conversation. 'Can you come and join me?' he told her, not acknowledging me.

'It's fine, I'll be here,' she said.

I tried to think of a way to defuse the situation. I didn't want him to think I was hitting on his girl. So I invited him to join us in the line. I stepped back so he could stand beside his girlfriend. He tried to talk to her, but she ignored him.

I had worked out what she was doing now, and I was inwardly cringing at her stupidity. Especially when she turned around and stood so she was facing me, her back to him. She opened her mouth to speak, but I wasn't listening. All my attention was on The Dude. What would he do? I decided that the smartest thing was to remove myself from the situation.

'Excuse me,' I said, and walked away to the back of the long line. I didn't care if it meant waiting longer for food.

I thought that would be the end of it. But no, this girl was persistent. She collected her food and then found me at the back of the line. 'What happened to you?' she said.

'I went to the toilet and didn't want to seem to be pushing into the line,' I lied.

'OK, I'll see you in the dining room,' she said.

Minutes later I entered the dining room through a back door and saw her sitting with her boyfriend. She had reserved a seat for me. She was looking around the room. I guessed she was looking for me.

I took a seat beside some boys and hoped she wouldn't see me. But dammit, she did. She smiled widely, got up and walked over to my table. 'Hey, what's up?' she said.

'I'll catch up with you later,' I replied. She didn't get the hint.

By now, The Dude was making his way over, and I could tell he was spoiling for a fight. No-one was going to invade his turf, especially not a refugee nobody. I sat there, bracing myself, expecting him to throw a punch at me. Instead, he pushed her.

She responded angrily, speaking to him in rapid Swahili. My guess is she swore at him.

I looked down into my food, my anger growing. I was trying hard to control myself, but I knew my composure wouldn't last very long.

Then she walked away. He knelt over me and grabbed me by my shirt collar. I pulled my head down, grabbing his hand and yanking it off me.

'My friend,' I said calmly. 'I hope you understand that I have nothing to do with your girlfriend. There's nothing between us.'

I was relieved when he said nothing and walked away. I hoped that would be the end of it.

But the girl wouldn't let it go. She found me again as I was on my way to soccer. 'What you did before wasn't very smart,' I told her. 'I'm sure you just want us to be friends, but I don't think your boyfriend is taking it that way.'

'I don't care!' she said. 'I've had enough of him. He's so controlling and I've had enough! I don't want to be with him anymore!'

'It has nothing to do with me,' I said. 'I can't help you. You take it up with him.'

As we were talking he came up behind us, grabbed her hand and dragged her away. They talked furiously. I hoped they'd leave me alone. I just wanted to play soccer.

He later found me again. 'So refugee, now you've taken my girlfriend,' he said. 'Who are you? You have nothing! This isn't your country. You can't come here and disrupt other people's lives!'

I tried to walk away. But he came up in front of me, blocking my path and pushing my chest hard. Then he pushed me again, harder, and I fell.

When he came at me again, I snapped. I stood up and swiftly punched him in the face.

He went down. The idiot. He didn't know what I was capable of. He didn't know I had trained to be a soldier.

I thought I must be in big trouble now. Surely the school wouldn't let me stay here. I went back to my dorm and began packing my things. By now, word of our exchange had got back to the teachers. One of them came after me, saw me packing, and said, 'What's wrong, David?'

'I don't want to talk, sir,' I said, still angry. 'I'm going back to the camp.'

'No, David. It's OK. I know what happened. We can sort this out.'

I was called into the headmaster's office. 'I want you to stay,' he said. 'We aren't going to punish you.'

The teachers must have known what they were dealing with. I sensed they were quietly pleased that The Dude had finally got what he deserved.

I returned to class the next day and sought out the girl who had started all the trouble.

'Have you broken up?' I asked.

She started ranting about what an arsehole he was but I cut her off. I suggested that the two of us hook up. I didn't even fancy her in that way. I just wanted to piss him off. And now, she was mine. I couldn't wait to break the news to him. I couldn't help but be cocky when I found him.

'Man, you don't know me and I don't know you,' I said. 'I'm not interested in us being friends. I hope you have learnt your lesson. I'm obviously a refugee, and there's nothing you can do to me. If you want to bring it on, I'm ready any time. But I advise you, you will get hurt. As for your girlfriend, she's now my girlfriend.'

I was trying hard to provoke him. I wasn't satisfied with punching his nose. I wanted to give him a good beating. But he said nothing.

I was too nervous to sleep in my own bed after that. Wide awake, I knew I could take on The Dude. But in my sleep—even in a state of half-sleep as I had been trained—I would be at a disadvantage. So for the next three nights, I put a blanket and pillow together to pretend there was a real person sleeping in my bed, and slept in the dining room.

But I had nothing to worry about. The Dude never bothered me again.

The girl and I hung out together for a few months. I treated her respectfully and I think she appreciated that. But I was missing life in Kakuma camp. I missed my boys. I wanted us to grow together, and I wished they had the same opportunities that I had been given.

Attending the school had been my first taste of normal life in the community, and it was scary. I knew the opportunities would be greater at the Kenyan school. I knew I'd have more food, a better education and more freedom.

But there was something comforting about being inside that fence, even though life was vastly tougher. Those boys were my brothers, and I felt safe with them. Tragically, the camp was the closest thing I had ever had to a home, and I was thoroughly institutionalised. I decided it was time to move back.

While the refugees struggled to survive on their food rations inside Kakuma, the Sudan they'd run from was in the midst of a crippling famine. Confronting images appeared in newspapers of people at a feeding centre—naked, starving and shockingly thin.

Meanwhile, Omar al-Bashir enhanced his own powers and officially became President of Sudan in 1993, after dissolving the Revolutionary Command Council for National Salvation.

Other nations became involved in the attempt to broker peace in Sudan. The Intergovernmental Authority on Development—an East African organisation whose members include Ethiopia, Uganda, Kenya and Sudan—attempted to search for solutions to end the war. But it had already persisted for a decade and the peace process would take years. There was no end in sight.

9

Girls and Riots

I resumed my career as a player. And not just of soccer.

There were two young ladies at the camp. They were both very smart. They had both been granted scholarships to attend a school outside the camp. They were both my girlfriends.

In my mind, it was normal to have multiple girlfriends. The two girls didn't know they shared a boyfriend. They wouldn't have accepted it. But if you were pretty good at hiding what you got up to, the situation was manageable.

With tens of thousands of people inside Kakuma camp, I could time it so that each girl never saw me with the other. I was managing it quite well. Until they began attending the same school.

Let's call them Jamila and Adeng. As they spent more time together at school, they became friends. One day, Adeng told Jamila she had a boyfriend. His name was David, and he was really good at soccer. She took out the photo of me that I had given her and proudly showed it off.

Jamila went quiet. She let the other girl continue bragging and giggling about her boyfriend, giving nothing away.

Then I received a letter from her. The camp's postage system was very unsophisticated. You'd go to church, and give your letter to someone that was bound to see the person you were writing to. The letters usually got to the intended recipient.

have anything to do with me. But Jamila didn't care what her family thought. I told her it was my intention to marry her; if I could find a better life and settle down I'd choose to do it with her.

For a while, I kept my promise of exclusivity. But then I couldn't help myself; I went back to picking up other girls. Jamila was always more special than the others. I always gave her more attention. I wrote her lots of letters and if we were at a function, I would stand beside her. I made it known to the other girlfriends that Jamila was Girlfriend Number One in the hierarchy.

She was a very special girl, the first person who stood up to me and told me to think about what I wanted to do with my life. She made me think twice about dedicating my life to soccer. I had been seriously considering a career as a professional soccer player, but there was no exposure here. It was impossible to imagine going from Kakuma refugee camp to the English Premier League.

I started thinking more deeply about my life and what I wanted because of her. She encouraged me to think of my education. She made me believe there was a future beyond Kakuma.

■

Over the years, we settled into the routine of the camp. By now, we had learnt to live with the unwavering emptiness in our bellies. We played soccer and went to our lessons and survived on our rations, while dreaming of the possibility of another life.

News would intermittently get back to us about what was going on in Sudan. A simmering tribal conflict was mounting in southern Sudan, and the ripples were felt as far as Kakuma.

A Dinka boy would hear that his mother had been killed during a village raid in Sudan by the Nuer people. That would be enough for him to clash with a Nuer boy in the camp. It compounded the bitterness that had lingered within all of us since the internal split in the SPLA. Soon, other Dinka and Nuer boys would join the fight, and it was like a football melee. Quite often, the boys throwing punches at each other didn't know what they were fighting about. The Kenyan police were called in, but they were too late. Many boys were killed in the riots.

It heightened the feelings of insecurity in the camp. The Dinkas far outnumbered the Nuer in the camp. After the riots, the Dinkas and the Nuer stayed away from each other. Most of the Nuer boys moved closer to the aid workers' compound for their own protection. But my Nuer teammates continued to stay with us. It was a brave move on their part, but we swore we'd protect them. I wouldn't have allowed other Dinka boys to touch them.

I hated all the conflict. Even as a teenager, I was thinking about peace. Most soccer teams in the camp were based on tribal lines. But my team was a rare tribal mix. We never talked about who came from what tribe. We made a deliberate decision to stay out of it. We were like brothers.

It took a long time for the camp to settle after the riots. You couldn't walk around at night alone out of fear you'd be attacked by another tribe.

Soccer matches were suspended for a while. It was too risky for Nuer and Dinka boys to be around each other. I felt sad about that; I thought that sport shouldn't distinguish between tribes.

The tension eased after a while, but the camp was still riddled with hostility. We went back to playing soccer, but we weren't playing with the Nuer boys.

I told my teammates one day that I was keen to play with a Nuer team again. I told them that we shouldn't be afraid to play with them.

The others seemed very cautious. Maybe I was being a little careless. I couldn't predict the consequences of playing with a Nuer team. But I thought it was a risk worth taking. I thought that soccer should be above all that tribal stuff. I was banking on the fact that my team was unique, because we had a tribal mix. I reasoned that the Nuer boys would not attack my team because it included Nuer boys. And they wouldn't want those boys to, in turn, be attacked by Dinkas. 'We can do this,' I told my teammates.

The boys respected me, and after some consideration they agreed.

I approached a Nuer team to play with us. In order for my gamble to work, we'd have to play on the Nuer side of the camp.

The game was set for Saturday. On Friday, we put up signs all over the camp, advertising our match. Other Dinka boys thought we were crazy. 'Why would you want to go and play there?' they said. 'It's so dangerous!' But my team backed me. We invited the aid workers to come and watch, and they thought the match was a good idea.

I decided to leave early and head alone to the Nuer compound. My teammates were resigned to my crazy ideas and didn't try to stop me.

A few hours before the game, I was greeted very warmly by the Nuer boys. They invited me to share a meal with them. Our time together proved to be an icebreaker. 'We're going to win,' I teased. I was confident that I had made the right decision.

It was a massive crowd. Dinkas turned up to watch the game in the Nuer compound, bringing clubs and sticks. I was slightly worried about how the crowd would behave. But I knew the players at least were above all that. We wanted to promote sportsmanship.

'If anyone kicks you, don't react,' I told my teammates. 'Let's just play soccer.'

It was a beautiful match. Both teams played skilfully. We won, and there were no riots. We safely returned to our side of the camp.

For me, it was a special moment, and not just because we won. It reinforced how sport can bring people together.

∎

The uneasy existence between the Dinkas and the Nuer continued. We lived together, but segregated.

We played another match with the Nuer boys in front of a packed crowd. I'm not a tall guy and, as a natural midfielder, I'm not great at scoring. But on this day, I scored my first ever header. Our boys roared and I celebrated like I was African soccer star Abedi Pele.

One more goal and we won. Seconds later I was flat on my stomach on the ground and blows were coming from all directions.

The Nuer spectators had run onto the pitch and were attacking all of us. Some of the players fought back and then ran off the field to safety. But I was in the centre of the ground and there were a pile of boys on top of me. I concentrated on protecting my face as about ten guys punched and kicked me.

Our Nuer opponents came to my rescue as soon as they saw me. They forced the boys off me and then surrounded me, forming a protective barrier against the crowd. I was unharmed. I shook their hands and thanked them as they escorted me off the ground.

I couldn't believe what had happened. But the next day, I was undeterred. I walked back to the Nuer compound. The way I saw it, the boys in the Nuer team were my friends. That was soccer. And I wasn't going to let tribal conflict drive a wedge between us.

My teammates thought I was crazy to return to the scene where I had been belted the previous day. But I felt there was a bigger picture; I was beginning to envisage what my country could be like without tribes at war with each other. I still felt bitterness towards the Arabs in the north, but I was thinking about what could be done to promote unity. The only way I could think of—for now—was through sport.

But then the conflict flared again. This time, it was amongst the Dinkas themselves. The Dinka Bor were pitted against the Dinka Bahr el Ghazal, which I'm part of. They were from the same tribe, but different states. I don't know what caused the fight. I think it was a basic misunderstanding between two guys that intensified into a punch-up. And then their friends got involved.

It got wildly out of control. Some boys used spears that they had made from tin. The Kenyan police were called in, but again they were too late. Huts were burnt down. And more boys were killed.

I never understood what that fight was about. As the tension lingered, my group made a deliberate decision to stay out of it. Our team was connected to the church, and that felt like the only safe place in the camp. The church was meant to be neutral territory.

Then the fight got uglier. There was a teenage girl from the same tribe as me, the Dinka Bahr el Ghazal, whose father was embroiled

I felt really bad when I read her letter. She wrote of how hurt she was that I hadn't told her the truth. I'll bet this girl isn't the only one, she wrote. I bet there are others.

She was right. There were others. I think there were about seven all up. My soccer skills had made me very popular with the girls.

Girlfriends for us weren't girlfriends in the Western way. There was no physical intimacy. We mostly hung out and talked, and even holding hands was a big step.

I really liked Jamila—more than all the others. I wouldn't have cared about losing the others, but I thought that Jamila was a keeper.

I began to write back to her, but couldn't find the right words. I knew she was right. My behaviour was indefensible. I thought the most strategic approach was to talk to her in person at church on Sunday. That was the only time we saw each other.

I arrived at church that Sunday to see my two girlfriends standing together. Adeng, still oblivious to our love triangle, introduced me to my other girlfriend. I told her that I needed to speak to Jamila. If Adeng suspected anything, she didn't show it.

'That's fine,' she said. 'I'll see you later.'

I told Jamila that I didn't want to write, that I wanted to tell her to her face how sincerely sorry I was. I told her she was right, there were other girls. I told her I would happily lose all the others, but I didn't want to lose her. I told her I'd tell the other girls it was over. If she agreed, I'd put the word out immediately.

She told me it was over.

I didn't give up. I set about telling the other girls I was no longer interested. I knew that my dumping the other girls en masse would get back to her. Then I wrote to Adeng and told her it was over. I told her I was with Jamila.

My strategy worked. Jamila took me back. But our newly exclusive relationship didn't go down very well with Adeng, who started a big catfight at school with Jamila.

Jamila's aunty later went off at me, accusing me of trying to ruin her niece's education—and her life. Her family didn't want her to in a fight with the Dinka Bor. He was slaughtered like a dog. Fearing for their lives, others from my tribe came to the church. Some of my friends and I were trying to help them.

The teenage girl came running towards us, seeking protection inside the church grounds. We let her inside the fence and told everyone to sit down and stay calm.

I was with my friend Peter, a Dinka Bor. As Peter and I shut the gate, a group of young Dinka Bor men carrying weapons charged towards us. They knew there were some Dinka Bahr el Ghazal hidden behind the gate. Being one of them made me a natural target. And my involvement in soccer made me an even bigger target, as my high profile in the camp meant that killing me would have caused more pain to my people.

Peter told me to go for my own safety. But I stood my ground. I told him I wasn't carrying a weapon. I wanted to wait and see what would happen.

The girl had watched her father get killed. Now, she wanted her revenge. She rushed forward, pushed open the gate and began running straight towards the men with the weapons. But it seemed to me that she'd only suffer the same fate as her father.

Peter and I ran after her. I stretched out and grabbed her just in time, just as the men with the weapons surrounded us. She was brave, and she fought me as I held her until she fell sobbing to the ground. I stood over her protectively as she cried. Peter stood beside me. Our priority was to save the girl.

The Dinka Bor guys recognised me 'Daudi, what are you doing?' one of them asked. 'Are you involved in this war?'

'No, I'm just here to hold back this girl,' I said.

They stood there for some time, and I held my breath. Then they backed off. 'Go back,' they said. 'And take the girl. We know you are not part of this war.'

They demanded to know who we were hiding inside. 'I'm happy for you to come and see for yourself they are women and children and they are scared,' I said. 'This is the only place where they can be safe.'

They believed me. I expelled the breath I had been holding and turned to walk back inside with Peter and the girl.

Lots of people were killed during the tribal clashes, and they were all taken to the cemetery near the camp. People turned up to the burials to express their anger at the deaths. The Kenyan police supervised, and insisted that victims from the warring groups be buried at opposite ends of the cemetery. Even in death, they were separated.

Tribal conflict is still raging in South Sudan. And it really shits me. What is the point of killing your own people? It's like raising your hand to your brother, then mourning his death the next day.

In 1996, Sudan held its first elections since the 1989 coup, and Omar al-Bashir remained president. Political parties had been banned since the coup and, according to the Inter-Parliamentary Union, no voting took place in eleven districts because of the continuing civil war in the south.

Human rights violations persisted. Amnesty International, in its 1996 report on Sudan, said that hundreds of suspected opponents of the government were detained 'without charge or trial'. It said: 'Political detainees were tortured and prisoners were routinely flogged as judicial punishment. Scores of children were abducted by paramilitary forces and hundreds of people were extrajudicially executed in the war zones.'

The Amnesty International report said that soldiers from the Sudan People's Liberation Army also committed human rights abuses, 'including torture and deliberate and arbitrary killings of captured prisoners and unarmed civilians'.

Meanwhile, the people of the south were subjected to another catastrophic famine in 1998. In July of that year, Médecins Sans Frontières reported that 120 people were dying daily due to starvation in Ajiep, in the province of Bahr el Ghazal in southern Sudan.

By the end of the decade, the government of Sudan had started exporting oil.

10

Death of Dreams

The camp transformed into a giant melting pot of human suffering. It expanded to accommodate the growing numbers of refugees fleeing all kinds of atrocities from different countries.

First, it was the Ethiopians and the Somalis. Inevitably, the dynamics of the camp changed. We could all relate to each other in some way. The instability in our respective countries had brought us all together.

It was very cramped. I can remember at one point walking past a sign that said there were more than 80 000 refugees living in Kakuma camp.

There were demarcations that placed people in different zones, and the camp effectively turned into three camps. Because the war persisted in southern Sudan, we far outnumbered the others.

By now, my eighteenth birthday had come and gone, unbeknown to me. I had become a man while inside the confines of a refugee camp—a decade after leaving my mama.

We began sharing our stories with our new neighbours. We lived together congenially most of the time, although there were tense moments. I can remember one significant fight between the Sudanese and the Somalis, but when you break it down it started with two kids fighting over something trivial. When their friends saw what was going on, they joined in and the fight intensified. The only people who knew the cause of the fight were the two boys who started it.

I was guilty of joining that fight, because I knew the Sudanese guy. But I continued to steer clear of the Sudanese tribal fights that still flared intermittently. I refused to let those fights stop me from seeing my Nuer friends.

The refugees from the other countries entered a camp that was vastly different to the one we had scratched out of the desert years earlier. The conditions had improved immensely, although there still wasn't enough food and we effectively remained prisoners.

The progress had taken years, but at least we could see it. The huts now provided greater insulation from the sun. The aid workers had found leaves that we wove together and placed on top of our plastic sheet roofs to provide coolness. We renovated our huts regularly, to the point where they eventually had roofs made from iron sheets.

There was a main hospital of a reasonable standard with beds and wards and doctors, aside from the smaller medical clinics scattered throughout different zones.

The schools had transformed too. When we first arrived at Kakuma, classes were held under a tree. Then we were given exercise books and we'd bring tins to sit on during class. Eventually, we built our own desks and seats from mud mixed with water, moulded into shape and left to dry. It was very clever—except that on the rare occasions it rained, our desks and chairs would be washed away and there'd be no classes for a while.

Then the aid workers gave us materials to build our own schools, similar to the way we had built our huts. We were so excited at the prospect of having real schools that it wasn't long before there were a number of them around the camp. Like the huts, they had mud-brick walls with plastic sheet roofs covered with leaves.

Then the real desks came—each made from a large piece of timber that three people shared inside overcrowded classes containing something like seventy or eighty kids in a class.

When the Somalis and Ethiopians came, they joined the camp's soccer competition. There were some highly skilled players among them. My team remained one of mixed Sudanese tribes. Then we recruited an Ethiopian guy. Despite still being known as Holy Cross, a Somali Muslim joined our team as goalkeeper. He wasn't fussed by our team's name at all.

The Kakuma camp's central soccer team also expanded to include refugees from other countries. We had a coach, Asafa, from Ethiopia. He was a lovely guy, and brilliant at soccer. He had played at a high level in Ethiopia before he was forced to flee his country.

Our team also had a new manager, a young man named Noriaki Takamura, who came from an organisation in Japan called the Wakachiai Project. He had come to Kakuma to run the sports in the camp. He was a great and compassionate man, and we became good friends.

Noriaki was very enthusiastic about soccer and our team's prospects. We were about to enter a national competition playing against other schools in Kenya. Asafa chose his best players and not only did I make the team, but the boys chose me as their captain.

We took it very seriously and trained hard. One of the challenges was learning the rules—such as yellow cards and red cards—to prepare us for a real competition.

Every afternoon, Noriaki came in his ute and brought us water, juice, bananas, oranges and other snacks. I had never been treated like a professional footballer before and it reinforced the importance of what we were doing. I felt that we weren't just playing for ourselves; we were playing for all the refugees. We walked with our shoulders back, chests out, determined to prove that we were just as good as the other teams.

Noriaki was very encouraging. I'd help him after training, chatting as we put away the equipment. I felt that he wasn't just doing his job; he truly cared about us. He would always bring us more food on the days we played. He didn't want us to play while we were starving. So on game day, the team would have rice and meat and vegetables. We had full bellies and felt like real footballers.

One day after a game, Asafa put his arm around my shoulder, and told Noriaki that he thought I was a game-changer. He said if anything could take this boy to the English Premier League, I'd fit in there.

It had never occurred to me that I was really good. We were poor refugee kids who had played soccer for the hell of it. Asafa gave us confidence, and made us believe that we could achieve anything.

■

We counted down the days to the national competition. The intense slog of training eventually slowed to a recovery pace. We walked around the camp pledging to do the refugees proud. They urged us to bring home the trophy.

Noriaki came looking for me and found me, a restless, nervous bundle of energy. 'David, I hope this will motivate you more. I want to tell you this because you're the captain,' he said. 'Once this competition is over, I want to talk to the Japanese government about taking you to play in Japan for a month or so. I also want to get you guys a few matches in London, so that the whole team can have exposure. David, I know the team will not come back, if you keep playing the way that you are. But let's worry about the issues with getting permission from the camp later.'

I didn't know what to say. I was so moved by the extent to which this man cared about me. To play in Japan and England was a dream. Unbeknown to us, Noriaki had been thinking about how to take us overseas, even though we had no passports and were effectively stateless young men. I quietly fantasised about playing for some of the biggest clubs in the world. My confidence surged. If this man believed so deeply in me, then I must be really good.

Later that night Asafa gave a long speech, telling us how proud he was of all of us. He urged us to remember what we had gone through. This was our chance to show people that we could rise above everything and play skilled soccer.

The next morning, Noriaki knocked on my door. 'David, are you still sleeping?' he said.

'No, I'm awake!' I replied.

He told me I would ride with him in his ute, along with Asafa and our friend Valentino, another refugee in the camp who worked with Noriaki to coordinate the sports. We had to drive to the town of Lodwar, a couple of hours away. Noriaki told me to make sure the others were on the bus, and we'd head off.

I rounded up the boys and they piled into the bus. Then I got into Noriaki's ute. We were about to drive off when one of the boys shouted: 'Bobby isn't here!'

Bobby was one of our strikers. Noriaki stopped the car and told me to get Bobby.

When I returned with Bobby, Noriaki said he had forgotten to get something. I got on the bus with the boys and we made the slow drive to the main gate. The ute would follow us.

We stopped at the gate so that security could go through our papers. It was a long and tedious process, and the boys were killing time by being rowdy and singing loudly and poking fun at each other. I grinned at their silliness and decided that travelling on the bus with my boys would be much more fun than driving in the ute.

So when Noriaki returned and poked his head into the bus, and told me to get in the ute, I happily told him I wanted to stay on the bus. 'Fine,' he said, 'we'll meet in Lodwar.' He got into his ute with Asafa, Valentino and some others.

Our bus driver was a friendly Kenyan who had watched us train. 'You guys are really good and passionate about soccer,' he told me as he pulled away from the compound.

We arrived in Lodwar with plenty of time to spare. We walked to the field, carrying our soccer balls. The place was packed and we were keen to show off our skills. We wanted the crowd to know that we had come to play.

A tense lump settled in my stomach as we waited for the others. I just wanted to get out there and play now. I was wasting nervous energy. I thought the ute had been right behind us, but it was taking longer than I had expected.

We must have been waiting for at least half an hour, because now the other boys were getting anxious. In the absence of our manager and our coach, they looked to me, their captain, for direction. But I didn't know what to do.

I was trying to come up with a plan when I noticed the police car. It must be extra security for the game, I thought, because of the massive crowd.

Two Kenyan policemen emerged from the car and began walking towards us. I willed them to keep walking past. But they stopped beside us.

'David? The captain?' one of them asked. I wondered how he knew my name. I didn't respond straight away. My mind was frantically exploring all the possibilities. Why would they want to talk to me? I couldn't stay silent forever. I made myself known.

'Please, we need to have a word with you,' he said.

The tension in my stomach had progressed to panic. I let the man take me aside as the others kept playing with their soccer balls.

'David, I have very bad news for you,' the policeman said. 'Your team manager's car was in an accident and there were lots of injuries . . . and I have the sad news that Noriaki died immediately.'

I tried to digest his words as tears silently rolled down my cheeks. The man put his hand on my shoulder, repeatedly saying my name. As I shakily sat down, the boys rushed over.

I couldn't speak to them. I was sobbing openly now. The others wanted to know what was wrong. I left it to the policeman to repeat his words. Valentino and Asafa had been injured, too, and had been taken to hospital.

I didn't bother asking the details of how it happened. I didn't want to know.

The boys were all crying now. I tried to think of what to do. I knew they would depend on me to take charge.

'David,' the policeman said, 'you are the captain. You have to coordinate your team and go back to the camp.'

I nodded, stood up slowly and walked over to the bus driver. By now, the word must have spread about why the match had been delayed. I looked into the crowd and saw faces that were sympathetic.

I tried to absorb the loss. Not only had my dear friend died, but all my dreams of playing soccer in England had died with him. There was no way that could happen now. I was also worried about my friends Valentino and Asafa. I had no idea how badly injured they were.

The bus driver gently placed his hand on my shoulder, whispering words of comfort and encouragement. I roughly wiped the tears off my face. I had to be strong for my team. We were in the middle of nowhere, and it was my responsibility to get them safely home.

I told the boys to collect their things and get on the bus. We were going back to camp. They glumly did as I said.

I stood outside the bus waiting for them to get in. I felt someone tap me on the shoulder. I turned around and was surprised to see the headmaster from the school I had attended outside the camp. He had come to watch us play.

'David, I'm really sorry to hear of your loss,' he said warmly. 'You're very courageous. What will you do now?'

I told him my team and I were going back to camp. He took my hand and I let him take me aside. 'David, I know you very well. You are a very good young man. I want you to play.'

What??? I was outraged. Our friend had died, and this man wanted us to play soccer!

I angrily tried to move away but he grabbed me and said: 'Why was your team manager coming to Lodwar? He put in so much time and invested in you guys. If he was alive, do you know what he would say? He'd say, "Go and play." That's the main reason you came here. You came to play.'

I realised he had good intentions. His words made me less angry, but they didn't change my mind. 'No, it can't happen,' I said. 'There's no way I can make the team play now. Look at them. Forget about me. They won't do it.'

'You can persuade them, David,' he said. 'Talk to them, and play for your manager.'

I started to think that maybe he was right. Noriaki had done so much for me. This was one last thing I could do for him. My challenge now was to persuade young men in pain to play.

The sombre atmosphere on the bus was in stark contrast to the boisterous mood in which we had left Kakuma. The boys were sitting in silence, waiting for me.

'Listen up, boys,' I said. 'What I'm about to say, none of you will agree with. But please hear me out.' I paused. 'We are playing.'

They all went nuts at me. Bele, a brilliant striker, stood up and angrily said, 'David, you are crazy!'

I waited for them to settle down and then repeated the headmaster's words. 'If Noriaki was alive, he would want us to play, and I know Asafa would want us to play too,' I said. 'Let's not play to win. Let's just play this one match and dedicate it to Noriaki.'

All I needed was for two or three guys to agree. If I could get just a couple of them on board, I knew the others would follow. And they did.

Once we told the authorities we'd play, they gave us some time to settle down and get ready. 'Take 30 minutes and let's grieve,' I told the boys. 'Then, when we hit that field, let's do what we do best. Play soccer. I want us to leave everything else behind.'

I stared at the grief-stricken faces of my teammates. Persuading them to play was one thing. But getting them to play with their hearts in the game would be something else. I was still struggling to contain my own grief. All I felt like doing was crying for Noriaki.

We started the game disastrously. My teammates played through their tears, as did I. By half-time, we were down two–nil.

No-one talked as we rested before the second half. I knew I had to find a way to motivate these guys. There was no point in playing for Noriaki if we were going to get a thrashing.

'All right, boys, I want you to choose one of two things,' I said. 'Either we go and play the soccer we used to play or we take off our boots and get back on the bus and go home. Everyone in favour of playing, let me know. I feel what you're going through, but this is not the soccer we are playing. Noriaki would be very unhappy with us.'

They said nothing. 'I want to go and play the game that I play,' I continued. 'If anyone else wants to play, let's go. Otherwise, let's get changed and go back to camp.'

Bele was the first to stand with me. The others followed. We returned to the pitch and played beautiful football—nailing victory with four goals.

■

Word of the accident had got back to Kakuma camp, as had the fact that we had played. The camp manager wanted to support and encourage us; he sent a worker to Lodwar with his blessing to keep going in the tournament, if that's what we wanted. We didn't hesitate. It had been a poignant victory, and we wanted to keep going for Noriaki.

We stayed in Lodwar that night in very basic lodgings. The next day, we travelled to a place called Kitale for our second match. The drive was much longer, taking several hours.

There, we played our brand of soccer—the soccer Noriaki had thought was good enough to pull us out of Africa and into a better life. We won.

Our winning streak continued as we travelled through Kenya over the next couple of weeks, playing different schools, progressing through the competition, not knowing how our friends in hospital were faring.

One day a woman arrived from Japan, representing the Wakachiai Project where Noriaki had worked. She introduced herself and told us she was here to support us. 'Anything you need, a big team is behind you,' she said. 'We want to pay our respects to Noriaki and this is the best way to do it.'

I was touched that she had come. I felt that we had so much to motivate us.

We made it all the way to the final in Nairobi. But our success came at a price—we picked up injuries along the way. I was among the injured; my right ankle had been knocked badly during a game and it was twisted and swollen. We went into the final with too many injured boys and no replacements.

I could barely run, let alone kick. But I had no choice but to play. We might have done very well had our team not been so riddled with injuries. We went down two to one.

We boarded the bus for the long ride home, tired and deflated. It was more than 700 kilometres from Nairobi to Kakuma, a drive that took around two days. Immersed in the euphoria of winning, we had been able to distract ourselves from our grief. But now that the competition was over, there was plenty of time to think about Noriaki.

And for me, there was ample time to think about how I had evaded death again—simply by choosing to travel in the bus instead of Noriaki's ute.

■

Noriaki's body was cremated and his family came to Kakuma for the service. They couldn't speak English and we couldn't speak Japanese, but it didn't matter. We connected through our shared grief.

I was relieved to learn that Valentino and Asafa were out of hospital and OK.

There was no soccer in the camp for a few weeks after our return. Maybe it was a way of paying our respects to Noriaki. I had lost all desire to play soccer. I didn't think it would take me anywhere now. Noriaki had made me dream of using soccer as a ticket to a better life, but that dream was dead.

Once again, my faith was tested. I started to question God. Why would He let this happen? He knew we were very poor, and Noriaki had been the only man who could have helped us. Why did God let bad things happen to good people? I didn't want to completely turn my back on God, but I had questions that no-one could answer.

Noriaki's death also put an end to the central camp soccer team. We went back to playing in our own teams. Noriaki had been the man who had brought us all together. When we lost him, we lost all incentive to compete.

When I did return to soccer, it was without passion. My game changed. I grew lazy, often skipping training. I felt that I had no future. I felt that my destiny was to stay there, surviving on food rations, with no opportunities. I was sure I'd be stuck in Kakuma Camp forever.

For many, the opportunity for resettlement came. What started slowly in the late 1990s gathered speed after 2000. Wealthy countries including the United States and Australia were accepting refugees from southern Sudan. According to the United Nations High Commissioner for Refugees Global Report 2000, *the UNHCR secured resettlement opportunities for almost 5000 Sudanese boys that year.*

Those who moved on to new lives sent money to their friends remaining in the camp, still waiting for their own chance.

Kakuma camp had transformed to the point where it was operating like a small city, with a population bigger than many large country towns. Small businesses were opening inside the camp, assisted by charities, and the tens of thousands of occupants could buy food and other goods using the money their friends had sent them. But they couldn't buy their freedom, and they remained in limbo.

Back in Sudan, Omar al-Bashir was re-elected president. According to the Inter-Parliamentary Union, it was the first election held under a new constitution that had removed a ban on political parties—a ban that had been in place since 1989. The IPU said that most of the opposition parties boycotted the election, as they had demanded it be postponed.

11

Better and Worse

The first time I watched television, I was a grown man.

Conditions inside the Kakuma camp had continued to improve over the years. Some people, aided by loans from charities, were clever enough to start their own businesses.

One Ethiopian man had a satellite television connected and began charging five shillings for viewings. He played movies and music videos. And for the first time, I got to watch a professional soccer match. I was mesmerised.

Wealthy countries were beginning to open their doors to Sudanese refugees on humanitarian grounds. Some of my friends were very lucky—they were given the opportunity to resettle in America. We had grown up together and we were like brothers. In the absence of parents, we had taken care of each other. When my friends left, they didn't forget those of us still suffering in the camp. They began to send us money. For the first time in my life, I had cash.

We began watching movies from America. The way we dressed and talked quickly changed. I grew dreadlocks, and we became 'homies'. With money in our pockets courtesy of our friends, we could buy clothes from the new businesses opening in the camp.

More than anything, I wanted to watch the English Premier League. Watching professional footballers influenced my own game. I had always relied on my instincts, but now I could learn from stars like David Beckham. I idolised him, and I loved Manchester United. We spent our weekends watching the games and then dissecting them, arguing over who had played well. The more games we watched, the more the standard of our own games improved.

We were given some money from Don Bosco to buy new uniforms. We argued over which jerseys to buy: Manchester United or Arsenal or Liverpool. The debate went on for two weeks and there was no winner—in the end we bought plain uniforms aligned with no team.

I was also inspired by black American movie stars like Denzel Washington and Wesley Snipes. They transported us to another life. It was an existence we could only dream of, where there was food whenever you wanted it and a real education and a job and money. I imagined what it would be like to live in a rich country like England or America. I wondered whether I'd get my chance to leave the camp. I really wanted to play soccer in England. But I wasn't fussy; I just wanted to get out of there.

It was agony, staying at the camp and watching the others get chosen to go to rich countries and exciting new lives. Then the letters came. Our postal system was slow but the mail usually got to us. The mail went to the main compound and the aid workers would pin your name on a board to indicate a letter had arrived.

My friend Awak was among the first to go with his family to Tasmania. He sent back photos of the beautiful Tasmanian landscape, so lush and green and unlike Kakuma. There were photos of him playing with white boys. The place looked wonderful, and I wished I was there with him. He was the first friend to send me money.

One of the charities began sponsoring some of the boys and girls who excelled at school to go to Canada. Our friends sent us letters about their amazing new lives, along with photos of themselves standing beside big cars and what looked like a mass of white powdered stuff that I had read about but never seen. It was snow.

There were photos of boys wearing nice clothes and shoes, sitting on real beds in nice houses. There was even a photo of a boy sitting on a motorbike!

I was happy for my friends. But each new letter accentuated my desperation to leave.

My hopes rested on a pinboard. Each week, new names were added to the pinboard. If your name was on it, it meant an interview, a medical check and the possibility of a plane ticket out of Africa.

The resettlement began mainly with families. Then children who were alone were chosen. First they were flown from Kakuma to Nairobi. Then they were flown to their new life. It was always special when the plane came to Kakuma to collect the next batch of refugees. We'd bid our friends goodbye, happy for them but envious too, and wondering if we'd ever see them again.

My great friend Dominic was among them. Soon after he left for America, he began sending me money. William Machok also went to America. We spent his last night in the camp together and, always thoughtful, he tried to console me. I was getting frustrated about watching my friends leave while I remained. He told me my time would come.

I didn't know how the names were chosen for the pinboard. It seemed so random. I wondered if they used a formula to determine whose circumstances were more hopeless.

As some of the boys from my soccer team began to leave, we had to recruit new boys. It wasn't the same. With fewer of my friends around now, and the loss of Noriaki, I felt very lonely.

Getting out of Kakuma became my obsession. As the months went on, I compulsively checked the pinboard for my name. But I never saw it. I slumped into a serious depression. I was so anxious that I would never get my turn. I'd never have the chance to do what other young men do—work, get married, have a family of my own. I'd be trapped here forever. I was still dating Jamila and fantasised about marrying her. But I didn't want to do that in a place like Kakuma.

The only bright side to my friends leaving was that so many of them were sending me money. Suddenly, money and food were not an issue for me. To supplement my food rations, I could buy meat and rice and vegetables.

It felt strange not being hungry. I had known hunger for virtually my whole life, and it was part of my identity. Even with money, I couldn't break the habit of having one meal a day, although it was much bigger and more nourishing. I ate more on the days we played soccer.

The departure of my friends made things better and worse—on the one hand I had money and more food, but on the other it was torture waiting for my turn to come.

The months went by, and the process began to slow. There were fewer and fewer names on the pinboard, until it seemed there were hardly any new names at all.

■

Rumours were going around of another way out. It was a difficult journey, quite expensive, and a very long way. But if you made it, you would get your chance.

There was a place called Ifo Camp in the town of Dadaab, close to the border with Somalia. It was set up mainly to cater to the refugees fleeing the civil war erupting in that country. Apparently, if you could get to Ifo Camp, the resettlement process from there was faster.

It was a very long drive from Kakuma to Dadaab. You had to travel to Nairobi first, then Dadaab. The journey was more than 1000 kilometres, about three days on the bus.

I wrote to my friends overseas, including William, and told them of my plans. They sent me money for the journey.

But it was trickier to get permission from the camp authorities to leave. I had no good explanation for going to Dadaab. I couldn't tell them I was leaving Kakuma with the intention of getting out of Africa.

Without written permission to travel, you could get into a lot of trouble with the Kenyan police. I asked one of the Kenyan bus drivers, a really lovely man, what I should do. By now, I could speak Swahili fluently and could easily converse with the locals. He told me that I was lucky; I looked more Kenyan than Sudanese, I could speak

Swahili, and I had money. And in Kenya, he told me, if you have money, you can bribe anyone who tries to stop you.

I thought about it some more. I had nothing to lose. I didn't tell Jamila of my plans. I decided that once I'd made it to Ifo Camp and got out of Africa, I'd work out how to get Jamila out, too.

So I packed my bag and walked out of the camp without any travel documents. I approached the bus driver and handed him my money. He told me there would be many roadblocks on the journey. The first two would be easy. If the police recognise that you are a Sudanese refugee, plead with them first. If that doesn't work, bribe them. But whatever you do, he said, don't pick a fight with them.

I took his advice. I was determined not to stuff this up. I got onto the bus and we took off for the short trip to the first roadblock. As he predicted, the bus stopped and some policemen poked their heads inside the bus and repeatedly called out in Swahili: 'Refugees! Refugees!'

I kept quiet, head down, pretending to be engrossed in my book. They didn't detect me, and gave the driver approval to continue. He drove away, giving me a sneaky thumbs-up.

I expelled my breath, only slightly relieved. There was still a long way to go, and many more roadblocks to test us. So much could still go wrong.

We pulled into the second roadblock. This time, the policemen ordered us to all get off the bus, form an orderly queue, and have our Kenyan identification ready.

I'd have to bribe them. I was the only foreigner, and waited at the back of the line for all the others to get on the bus.

When it was my turn, a policeman spoke gruffly to me in Swahili. 'Where is your identification?' he asked.

'I don't have any travel documents,' I nervously responded in Swahili.

'Are you Kenyan?' he asked.

I shook my head no.

'Where did you learn to speak Swahili?' he asked.

'In the camp,' I replied.

He pulled me aside to an outdoor office. My heart sank as I heard him tell the bus driver to drive off without me. I wouldn't even make it past the second roadblock.

The bus driver was a good man, and he tried really hard to help me. He got off the bus and pleaded with them on my behalf. I tried to offer the policeman money. But he wouldn't be bribed. I was hand-cuffed and forced to sit alone while they talked about me as though I wasn't there. I didn't dare defy them. I was petrified.

As they took my bag, the bus driver had one last quiet word to me. He looked at my forlorn face and said, 'David, this is the first try. Never give up.'

They left me sitting there for two hours beneath a tree. I hadn't eaten in hours. But they didn't offer me food. They took it in turns to mock me, telling me I was a refugee, that this wasn't my country.

I silently endured the humiliation, feeling that the situation was hopeless. If I couldn't get to Dadaab then I might as well return to Sudan.

Later that evening they pushed me into a police car and drove me back to Kakuma, where they uncuffed my aching wrists and told me not to pull a stunt like that again.

■

My misery grew as the months dragged on. I still hadn't seen my name on the pinboard and I was on the verge of giving up.

I wrote to William again. This time he sent even more money, so that I could offer bigger bribes

I planned another bus ride. This time, the first two roadblocks pre-sented no problem. I offered the policemen money and they didn't argue with me. By now, the Kenyan police had learnt that many Sud-anese refugees were trying to get out of Africa via Dadaab, and they had figured out that it was a good way for them to make some extra cash.

My confidence was growing as we pulled into the third road-block. I was sitting near the back of the bus, trying to be invisible.

I held my breath and hoped this roadblock would go the same way as the first two.

The driver got off the bus and told the policemen there were no Sudanese people on the bus. Even while I was silently appreciating the driver lying for me, the men were peering into the bus. One of them eyed me and stopped. I tried to look as though I was supposed to be there.

'I want to see your Kenyan ID,' he snapped.

'I don't have one,' I said.

'Are you Sudanese? Get out!'

There were a few people standing in front of me on the bus. Wading through them as I politely asked them to move slowed down my exit.

The moment I stepped off the bus, one of the cops grabbed me and shoved me. 'Why did it take you so long to get out?' he shouted.

He had pushed me so hard that I had fallen onto the dusty ground. All the anger and frustration that I felt mounted at once, and I lost it. I stood up and swiftly punched the cop in the face.

It was an effective blow, and sent him sprawling on the ground, his gun falling in the other direction. I don't know what I was thinking, but I ran for the gun. I wasn't quick enough; the other cops caught me and beat me and beat me until I passed out.

■

I woke in a filthy cell, reeking of piss. The cell was divided into two—one side was for peeing and shitting, the other was where you sat and awaited news of what was going to happen to you. The arseholes had thrown me into the piss and shit end.

I slowly regained consciousness, grimacing as I realised where I was. They had taken my belt and shoes and shirt, so all I wore was my trousers. They had taken my bag and money, too.

The stench was revolting. I tried to walk to the other end of the cell, but my cellmates yelled at me to stay away. 'You stink, man!' they shouted.

I lost it, hitting anyone who tried to stop me from moving to the less smelly end of the cell.

There was another Sudanese man in there. Despite my stench, he grabbed me and tried to protect me from the others, and urged me to calm the hell down.

'I know you. You're David,' he said. He was in there because he'd refused to bribe a policeman. His name was Atem. I didn't know him, but he had recognised me from soccer.

'What happened?' he asked.

I told him everything. The others listened too, as I told them of how the policeman had pushed me, so I had punched him. They were all impressed by that bit. It's easy to make friends in a police cell when you've just punched a policeman.

'Hey, you did so well,' said a big guy. 'You can sit here next to me and no-one will touch you.'

We were brought food, but it looked like it had been marinated in filth. I didn't touch it.

I was incarcerated in there for a few days, not eating the whole time. I waited for the morning when the big boss would come in and tell me to write my statement and tell me my case would be heard.

I walked into his office, starving and smelly, shirtless and barefoot. The big boss sat down and began writing. I stood quietly in front of him until he put his pen down and stood up and looked at me closely.

He kept staring at me, not speaking. I decided that my best strategy was to be stubbornly silent. I was determined that he would be the one to break the silence.

Then he did something unexpected. He laughed. 'Aren't you that soccer player from the camp?' he asked.

I was taken aback, but hopeful. 'Yes,' I mumbled.

'Wow. I've watched your games a few times,' he said, sounding almost friendly. 'What happened?'

I told him the whole story, not leaving out the way the policemen had treated me.

He listened thoughtfully. 'All right, you sit there,' he said. 'Where are his clothes?' he shouted outside the room.

Someone came in with my clothes. 'Where's your money?' he asked as I got dressed.

'I don't know, sir,' I replied.

'Where is David's money?' he shouted again. There was no answer.

He walked out of the room and I could hear him demanding to know where my possessions were. But no-one was forthcoming. I bet they had taken my stuff.

He came back into the room. 'David, the best I can do is take you back to Kakuma,' he said. 'I'll get a car. Before that, go shower.'

He gave me some clean clothes and I showered and put them on, and he said, 'Let's go to town.'

We drove to a restaurant and he ordered some food. I hadn't eaten in days. As I wolfed the food down, he said he'd take me to Kakuma himself, as he had a meeting there.

We drove back to the police station first, and I asked if I could talk to the man that I had punched. He agreed to meet me.

'I'm really sorry,' I told him. 'I lost it because you pushed me.'

'It's OK,' he said. He and his friends must have thought they got lucky that day. I would have had at least 4000 Kenyan shillings on me.

As the big boss later drove me back to the camp, he told me to tell him everything about myself. When we pulled into the camp, he told me he'd come back and see me tomorrow.

I didn't know what to do next. I felt bad about bothering my friends for more money when I kept getting busted. I had all but given up on getting to Dadaab.

The man kept his word. He returned the following day with gold in his hands: a permission slip from the camp that said that I was going to visit relatives in Nairobi. I'd be able to travel legally now. From Nairobi, there would be no trouble getting to Dadaab.

I was touched that he had decided to help me. I boarded a bus to Nairobi and had the smoothest journey I'd ever had. I was feeling calm and actually enjoyed the long ride. The dusty landscape was quite

This was my first home in Australia, the housing commission flat in Fitzroy where I lived with my cousins. I still had my dreadlocks!

Where my life journey began, at the community housing in Toorak where I lived for two years. The place is called Armagh and it is run by Initiatives of Change Australia. My life underwent a huge transformation after I attended the Life Matters course.

This is Visier Sanyu from the National Council of Churches. He is the man who introduced me to Initiatives of Change Australia. He is still my very good friend, and played a significant role in helping me to change my life.

This is Kelly Fern, who I met while she was working at the National Council of Churches. She was very welcoming and one of the first white people I became close to. After all, we are all equal human beings.

At the Great Ocean Road, my first ever trip to the beach, and finally letting go of the dreadlocks. I decided that it was necessary. If I was to become a role model and peace activist I had to look smart! This was also when I began volunteering at the Breakfast club, and I thought it was important that the kids saw me differently.

Having a laugh with my friend Shane after greeting then–Immigration Minister Kevin Andrews with my white face and vegemite sandwich! (Image © Penny Stephens / Fairfax Syndication)

The team that started the Sudanese Youth for Reconciliation and Hope. It was our first meeting between the north and south of Sudan. It was very significant, and I will cherish this moment forever. We attempted something that not even the political leaders of the north and south did, and it was a huge achievement.

The core team behind the Sudanese Youth for Reconciliation and Hope—standing from left: Cheryl, Akec, Biong, Ahmed, Deng and Yousif. Sitting: Faten, me, Ola and Athieng. I'll always hold this team dear to my heart. One day I'll resume these dialogues again between the people of the north and south.

beautiful. I imagined that I would get to Ifo Camp, fill in an application form, spend a few weeks there and then I'd be off to America. It would be that easy.

■

Many others had had the same idea. And they thought it would be easy, too. So when I finally arrived in Dadaab after three days and an uneventful bus ride, I was gutted.

The place was a nightmare. It took me back ten years, to when we had first arrived at Kakuma and it was empty and filthy.

The first Sudanese who had made the trek from Kakuma to Dadaab had been lucky—I heard that some of them did manage to get out. But there were so many Sudanese here now. And I soon learned with a sinking heart that the resettlement process from here would be no easier.

Some of my friends were here, too. Because of the way we had arrived, we were not registered as refugees in Ifo Camp. That meant we weren't entitled to the food rations provided. We would have to buy our own food with the little money we had.

I couldn't believe how unlucky I was. I thought things would be better here, that I'd finally get my ticket out.

Disease and starvation and death drifted through the congested camp. Ifo Camp was nowhere near as advanced as Kakuma, which seemed civilised in comparison with its schools and businesses and television.

There were fierce clashes between the Sudanese and the Somalis, who blamed us for slowing down the resettlement process out of Dadaab. I think that some of them believed that they would have got out sooner had Sudanese refugees not crashed their camp.

The Sudanese were placed in a compound with a large fence around us. It felt like being back in a detention centre all over again.

One day, my friends and I went on the long walk to the toilet area in the bush. We did our thing and then as we walked back, we were surrounded by men with guns. They demanded that we hand over everything we were carrying and our clothes. I don't know who they were, but they looked like they wouldn't hesitate to use their guns. So I gave them what they wanted. I was relieved that I didn't have much money on me; I'd left most of it in the camp.

We walked back nearly nude, and my spirit was completely broken. I had tried so hard to make things better. Now, I couldn't see beyond this nightmare.

But there was an end. The authorities eventually decided to transport the refugees from Ifo Camp to Kakuma. By now, I'd been here for a few months. I couldn't believe that after everything, I was literally being driven back to the place I had tried so hard to escape.

But I was relieved, too. The conditions at Kakuma were First World compared to this. So when the buses arrived to take us to Kakuma, I was happy to see them.

We drove non-stop for three days. Nothing had changed at Kakuma. I found Jamila and told her what had happened. She had been worried about me, but she understood that desperation drove you to do whatever you could to better your life.

I was happy to see my friends again, but I couldn't get over the sadness. The sadness quickly transformed into a serious depression. I stopped playing soccer and lost all desire to do anything.

■

My cousin Archangelo was resettled in Australia in 2002. I didn't know it then, but I was twenty-four years old by that stage, and had lived in Kakuma for ten years.

There were always rumours around the camp about ways to get out. The latest rumour was that if you had a relative in a country like Australia, they could send you a form to sponsor you. That strengthened your chances of being accepted by that country.

But I was giving up hope, and considering going back to Sudan. I had heard that people had spotted my father in his village of Turalei.

Archangelo wrote to me regularly, and sent me his email address. I didn't have email, but I asked a worker if he would email Archangelo for me.

'Tell him that I'm OK, that life is OK, but I think I'm going to go back to Sudan,' I said. 'I want to find my parents in the village and see what is happening there, because I don't think anything is going to change here. I don't think I'm ever going to get out. I wish Archangelo the best and thank him for sending me his letters.'

The worker did as I asked. The following day he had a response. He printed out the email and handed it to me.

My cousin told me not to give up, and to have hope. He said he'd send some forms from Australia and I'd have to fill them in and send them to the Australian High Commissioner in Nairobi. Then I might be able to come to Australia.

It was the tiniest glimmer of hope I'd had in a long time. I filled in the forms and sent them, along with some passport-sized photos— because by now you could even get your photo taken in Kakuma.

Archangelo warned me that it would take a very long time. You will need to be patient, he said.

I sent off my application and tried to forget about it. But I was so hopeful that I even started playing soccer again.

After years of intermittent negotiations, a ceasefire was finally agreed upon in Sudan. President Omar al-Bashir met with Sudan People's Liberation Army leader John Garang de Mabior and, with the help of the United States of America, they agreed to the Sudan Peace Act in 2002. By then, Riek Machar had rejoined the SPLA.

The Act aimed to find solutions to end the war in Sudan. It was signed by then–US President George W. Bush, and required the government of Sudan to negotiate with the SPLA in good faith, or face the threat of sanctions. However, the agreement was fragile, and negotiations would continue for years.

And a new crisis would emerge. In 2003, rebel groups in Darfur in western Sudan took up arms against government forces, citing neglect and oppression of the region. Local people feared for their lives and fled Darfur, seeking refuge in Chad. Then–United Nations Secretary-General Kofi Annan declared the situation a humanitarian crisis, and cited reports of murder, rape and the burning down of entire villages. As the conflict persisted over the years, there were at least tens of thousands of deaths—although some estimates put the numbers at hundreds of thousands.

12

The Long Road to Safe

I had spent years returning hopefully to the pinboard. One day, I finally saw my name on it.

It was 2004, almost two years since I had applied to go to Australia. I had been in Kakuma Refugee Camp for twelve years. I was twenty-six years old.

I had spent all my childhood and adult years running away from war and living in refugee camps. I had never had the chance to be a child at all.

I was playing soccer one day when a guy told me he had seen my name on the pinboard. I did not dare hope. It was dark, but I rushed to the board anyway, bringing a torch with me.

I shone my torch onto the pinboard. Sure enough, there was my name. I walked away in disbelief, only to return and double-check, torch beaming onto the board. Yep, that was my name.

It was only the first step, and there were no guarantees. But still, I felt the glow of excitement. I had been granted an interview with someone at the Australian High Commission. I was told to collect my travel permission to leave the camp and get the bus to Nairobi.

My cousin Archangelo had also applied to sponsor his brothers Boing and Tiel, and his sister Adakchin. I would join them in Nairobi.

I found Jamila and told her my news. We didn't say goodbye,

because we thought we'd see each other again. I assumed that after my interview I'd return to Kakuma, where I would await the outcome.

I packed a small bag, including the photo of Emmanuel and me. Then I headed, with my dreadlocks still intact, to the office in Nairobi.

'You can't go to an interview with an important Australian man looking like that!' my friends had warned me. 'He'll think you're a criminal!' But I wasn't going to ditch the dreadlocks. I brushed off accusations that my dreadlocks would jeopardise matters for other refugees.

I walked into the office in Nairobi, slightly intimidated. A white man stood up and extended his hand. I shook it as he looked at me, smiling kindly.

'Hi David, how are you?' he asked, gesturing to me to sit down. 'I like your dreadlocks. They're cool!'

I relaxed instantly. He was well dressed in a suit and tie. He asked me if I wanted water or tea. I politely declined.

'David, would you like an interpreter?' he asked.

'No, sir,' I said.

He laughed. 'David, you are the first confident guy I've met. Are you refusing an interpreter? Do you understand what I'm saying?'

'Yes, sir,' I replied.

'Tell me your name again, and tell me your story,' he said.

I was silent.

'Go on,' he said encouragingly. 'Tell me your story.' And he put down his pen and leaned back in his chair. 'If it's very hard, I'll get an interpreter for you.'

I remained quiet for a while. I didn't know where to start. 'Sir, I'm thinking what can I tell you? My story is very long,' I said.

He laughed again. 'I have all day,' he said.

So I gave him an overview of my story, leaving out quite a lot. He listened, not once interrupting.

'Thank you, David,' he said when I had stopped talking. He picked up his pen and scribbled in his notebook.

'Good luck,' he said. 'Hopefully you will go to Australia. Do you know anything about Australia?' I said no.

'Do you want to go to Australia?' I said yes.

When I emerged, my cousins were worried. My interview had taken longer than usual. They assumed that meant that I had done badly in the interview. But I was confident. I told them of our long conversation, and of how he had wished me luck and hoped I'd go to Australia. That, I thought, was a very good sign.

■

I had been wrong about returning to Kakuma. After the interview, we stayed in Nairobi, in a place where other refugees were staying, while we waited to learn of our fate. We had food and a comfortable place to sleep. There was a strong security presence, and we weren't allowed to leave the hotel. In any case, I didn't want to. I was so close now that I didn't want to do anything to stuff things up. I spent the time sleeping and reading books and waiting.

And then our letters arrived, hand-delivered by a Kenyan man. I tore open the envelope and found a letter of acceptance, a visa and travel documents. I read the letter over and over. I couldn't believe it. I was going to Australia forever. All four of us would go together.

I immediately thought about Jamila. We had never said a proper goodbye. I knew she was the girl I wanted to be with. I was worried that I'd never see her again.

I started to write her a letter. I wanted to tell her everything, how much she meant to me, that I was no longer a player, that maybe I could sponsor her to come to Australia.

But I didn't need to send her the letter. While I had been waiting in Nairobi, she had started the process of going to another country. As luck would have it, she came to Nairobi while I was still there.

She came looking for me. We organised a time to meet up, and I asked a guard if it was OK if we left the hotel to go to the restaurant across the road. I had no money, so she paid. We spent hours talking and making plans. I wanted to clear the air. So I told her about the other girlfriends. I told her they didn't mean anything to me. I told her that I loved her, that I wanted to marry her, and that I'd try to find my parents to get their permission. Then I'd seek her parents' permission.

I think she believed me. She told me she had cousins in Australia, so she'd be able to find me. We wished each other good luck and hugged; I kissed her on the cheek and said goodbye.

■

It didn't take long to pack. I wore shorts and a shirt, carrying a jumper in my bag because it was August, and I had been warned it would be freezing where I was going. The only other possessions I owned in the world were a pair of pants and my precious photo of Emmanuel and me. I had no money.

We had an evening flight. The bus came to our lodgings and drove us and some other refugees to Jomo Kenyatta International Airport. I was still in a state of disbelief. I thought that, any moment now, the bus would turn back to Kakuma and some guy would tell us the whole thing had been one big misunderstanding.

We continued the drive to the airport, walked into the building and began the strange process of checking in. Our almost-empty bags were placed in a machine that I was told would screen the bags and send them to the plane. I worried about being separated from my bag but didn't want to risk making a fuss and being told I couldn't get on the plane.

So I let my bag go and joined another line. I couldn't help but notice that others in the line were carrying passports. All we had was a piece of paper with our names and photos. I worried again that our papers wouldn't be good enough. My goal was to get on that plane, and I was terrified that someone would try to stop me.

A man at the counter asked me which city I was going to. I had no idea. All I knew was that I was going to Australia. He typed something into his computer and printed out a ticket and told me I was going to Melbourne. That was a very good place, he said. We would fly to Johannesburg first, then on to Australia.

Even with my ticket in my hand, I still waited for something to go wrong. But the four of us got on the plane without incident, found our seats and sat down.

Now, I discovered a new fear. How safe were these planes? And how would this plane get up into the sky? I hoped we wouldn't crash and die before we got to Australia. But that fear was superseded by the fear that someone would find us on the plane and tell us to get off. I was so nervous. I just wanted the plane to take off. 'Relax, man!' my cousin beside me said.

Then someone began talking into a loudspeaker and I thought that was it, someone was going to call out my name and tell me to get off the plane. But no, it was just some girls in nice uniforms doing a safety demonstration. I leaned forward in my chair, trying not to give away my anxiety. Then I could feel the plane begin to move. I was so afraid of the plane moving, but I was even more afraid of the plane never ever leaving.

Then we were up in the air. I didn't take my seatbelt off for the whole flight, even when the seatbelt sign was switched off. I was busting to pee but didn't dare move. I thought if I did something stupid, the plane would stop and they'd make me get off.

The well-groomed ladies in the uniforms came around and offered us warm towels. I said no thanks. When they later came around with food, I also declined. I didn't want to be presented with a large bill at the end of the flight when I had no money.

'Are we supposed to eat?' I asked one of my cousins.

'The food looks strange, anyway,' he said.

One of the flight attendants came back and told us we had to eat. We were going a very long way, she said. Besides, the food was all free.

My cousins and I exchanged looks and said we'd love some food. It looked strange when it arrived. I picked up the bread and had some juice and the rice. But I didn't recognise the green vegetables and I had never seen cheese before. I wasn't brave enough to try it.

I really didn't like the food, so when the flight attendant came around offering more, I said no. I wrapped the blanket around myself and slept for hours. I didn't eat again for the entire journey to Australia.

■

We flew into Sydney first. It was dark, and as the plane hovered over the city, I thought it was so beautiful. The city lights glittered as the plane made its descent. There must be something burning down there, I thought.

Going through immigration had been surprisingly smooth. I thought they might still send us back to Africa. But instead, the white people welcomed us to Australia.

We changed planes for the last time that night, and headed to Melbourne and our new lives. I couldn't wait to see my cousin Archangelo, the man I had to thank for making this happen.

We touched down in Melbourne and walked through the exit at Tullamarine Airport. The doors to my new city opened and a shock of chilly air hit my face. Man, I had never felt so cold! I winced and bolted back inside the terminal, wondering how it was possible to be warm inside and so cold outside. I put on my jumper before braving the cold again.

In the distance, I saw my cousin. We happily ran to each other. Archangelo had brought along a huge welcome party of strangers. When I saw my fellow Sudanese people beaming at me, looking as though they belonged here, I knew I had found safety at last.

According to Immigration Department figures, there are more than 25 000 Sudan-born people living in Australia. The department's Sudanese community profile, published in 2007, says that Sudan-born migrants that came to Australia before 2001 included skilled migrants.

Since 2001, the report says, the large increase in the Sudan-born population in Australia was a result of the humanitarian program. More than 98 per cent of the Sudan-born people living in Australia came here through this program, as a result of the civil war. Most of them identify as Christian, and the main languages spoken by them are Arabic and Dinka. The largest communities are in Victoria and New South Wales, and they mostly live in capital cities.

As they settle into their new lives without war, they soon find their new home comes with other challenges.

13

Becoming a Real Person

The car stopped unexpectedly. Through my tiredness, and while struggling through the unfamiliar sensation of jetlag, I noticed that the cars around us had stopped, too.

'Why are we stopping?' I asked.

'See those red lights there?' Archangelo said. 'We have to stay here until the lights turn green. Then we can move.'

Wow. I had only just arrived in Australia, and already there were things about this country that I found amazing.

I was totally impressed that Archangelo had a car. We had piled into it and driven out of the airport's multiplex carpark. I was fascinated by the levels upon levels of cars, the machine where you inserted money, and the thing that automatically lifted to let you out of the carpark.

By the time we pulled up at a tall building with lots of flats, it was very late at night. But inside, there were more people waiting for us, all Dinkas. And there was a feast.

I walked into the flat. 'Whoa!' someone said. 'How did you get to Australia with dreadlocks? Did you go to your interview with those things?'

I was tired, but still wanted to stay up and speak to the elders in my new country. They talked about life in Australia. They told us that this was a nice country and life was good here. You could get anything you wanted. But they told us that some boys had come to Australia and immediately got lost, getting sucked into alcohol, and getting into trouble. 'Set your goals now and embrace the opportunities,' they said.

We stayed up until 3 a.m. While the women sang songs, a small celebration was taking place inside my heart.

The flat was tiny and I had to share a bed with my cousin. I didn't care. As far as I was concerned, I was in paradise. I couldn't sleep, and not just because of the jetlag. I stayed up all night, staring out the window, gaping at my new city.

■

On my first day in Melbourne, I learnt that I was staying in something called a housing commission flat on Brunswick Street, in a suburb called Fitzroy near the city.

I wanted to spend the day exploring my exciting new city. Archangelo said the first thing we had to do was go to a place called Centrelink, so the Australian government would know we existed.

We travelled on a train to a suburb called Footscray. We walked into the Centrelink building, and were greeted by a friendly man.

'Welcome to Australia,' he said. 'I'm sure you will like it here. It will not be like where you came from. Here, there are lots of opportunities and it's up to you to decide what you want to do with your life.'

He told us we'd have to open bank accounts. I wondered where I'd get money to put in the bank. Archangelo told me that Centrelink would give me money, and automatically put it in the bank for me. 'You have to decide if you want to study or work,' he said.

Wow, I thought. This country is amazing. They just give you money for free. I wondered where the money came from. Maybe the government had a factory in a secret location where they made money all day, and then gave it to people.

I was now officially registered as a real person in this country. We headed back to our flat. As we walked up Brunswick Street, a black man approached us, extended his hand and said: 'Welcome, bro. This is your country.'

I thanked him. I was touched. I told Archangelo there must be lots of African people here. He said no, these people were Aboriginal, the first Australians and the original landowners of this country.

'But isn't this a white man's land?' I asked.

I'd never heard of Aboriginal people before. It made me want to read more and learn about them.

Our next stop was the Catholic church nearby, where Archangelo introduced me to Father Patrick. I immediately warmed to him. 'What are you guys doing tomorrow?' he said. 'I'll take you to Healesville Sanctuary, where you can see the native animals.'

I couldn't believe how nice everyone was. It was chilly the next morning when we went to the church to meet Father Patrick. I was wearing pants and a shirt. I didn't own a jacket. Father Patrick took one look at me and went back into the church, emerging with a black leather jacket.

'Try this on,' he said. It was warm and comfortable and fit perfectly.

It was a beautiful drive to Healesville. I finally got to see the kangaroos I had read about in Kakuma.

When we got back to Melbourne I tried to return the leather jacket. But Father Patrick wouldn't let me. I still have it to this day.

■

Before we had arrived in Australia, Archangelo had contacted the Office of Housing about organising a place for us to live. There were about ten of us sharing his cramped flat, and it wasn't sensible or sustainable in the long term. Archangelo took us to the Office of Housing and, within a few weeks, the four of us had another flat in the same building. He was on level five. We were on level eleven.

Our flat had three bedrooms and no furniture. The walls were white and clean. There were broken windows, the toilet was stained, and some of the carpet had burn marks. But to me, it was like a palace.

The woman from the Office of Housing told us to contact the Salvation Army and they'd help us with furniture. The next morning, they came over with four brand new single beds and a fridge.

As we unwrapped our beds, I couldn't help but think again that this country was amazing. You simply told people what you needed, and they gave it to you.

I couldn't sleep that night in my new soft bed. I still couldn't believe this was real. I kept thinking that I was going to wake up and find that I was back in Kakuma, and the whole experience had been a dream. I thought someone would storm into my room screaming: 'Wake up! I hope you enjoyed your holiday. Time to go back to Africa now!'

■

We were assigned a social worker at the Fitzroy Learning Network, a centre for asylum seekers and refugees to socialise, where there were computers and volunteers prepared food. Our social worker was Sara, a woman who radiated kindness and intelligence and smiled frequently. We told her we had a flat and beds and a fridge, but we needed some sheets and blankets and a couch and kitchen utensils. She organised everything.

She took us shopping. When we first walked into Safeway, I was astonished at the size of the place and the aisles and aisles of groceries. She explained how to read the labels on food, and how to find things.

She taught us about eating a nutritious, balanced diet. I was used to eating anything I could find to fill the emptiness in my belly. Nutrition had never entered the equation.

She showed us lots of strange-looking flowery things. One was green and was called broccoli. I'd never seen it before. I wondered, do people actually eat this?

I walked down the aisles until I came to shelves full of things for pets. I couldn't believe there was a whole section devoted to stuff for animals. It seemed that the dogs in this country enjoyed more food than I had had in Kakuma. I thought about all the dogs I'd seen since I'd arrived, how they'd been cuddled by people. And I thought that people treated their dogs in Australia vastly better to the way we had been treated in Ethiopia.

That night, I had a house with a full fridge. I couldn't believe that anytime I wanted food, all I had to do was walk to the fridge and get it.

I had moved into a very different world, and was slowly getting acquainted with the things I had only read about or seen on television. Sara showed us how to use the oven in our flat. I was a bit nervous about using the oven. While I was still in Kakuma, I'd heard stories about people in their new countries trying to use the oven and almost burning the house down. The first few times I attempted to cook rice I managed to burn it, and the smell of smoked rice filled our flat.

Sara had organised a television and a couch for us. By now, the money from Centrelink was in my bank account. But I didn't think that I had done anything to earn it. In my mind, you were given money in exchange for work. What kind of place gives you money for not doing anything?

I prayed for almost an hour before going to bed that night. I thought of my friends who were still in Kakuma, and hoped they would get the opportunity to come to this nice place. I hoped that I could start working to make enough money to send to them. And I thanked God for everything.

But I couldn't sleep. Arriving in Australia and immediately having everything had not brought instant relief. I had carried the heavy burden of pain and hatred since I was eight. And I couldn't shrug it off.

When you're plunged into a desperate situation and running on the adrenaline that survival demands, there's no time to dwell on what you're going through. All you can think about is where your next meal will come from, as you prep yourself to react to any situation. I had grown up surrounded by people whose suffering was equal to mine. Our pain was locked away, unheeded, because indulging any feelings of depression could kill you.

Once you're in a safe place, and life is less urgent, suddenly there's time to think. And now, I couldn't stop thinking about everything. Images that had been stockpiled in my head flickered non-stop like a slideshow. Things I had done. Things I had eaten. Things I had seen. Things that had happened to me. Images of people dying in front of me, and of burying their bodies.

I could clearly remember the time I had watched three men get blown away, killed by a firing squad. The men had each committed a crime. We had all been called in to watch. Some of the other boys sitting around me had closed their eyes. But mine were wide open.

The first two men fell to their deaths immediately. But the third took longer. He fell onto his knees first, staring out at us as about nine men fired at him. Then he moved forward and slowly fell to his death.

Why bother killing them, I wondered? Why not just give them guns and send them to the front line? They probably would have died anyway.

I kept thinking and remembering and couldn't find the off switch to my brain. I tried to calm my head by reminding myself that I was far away from all that now. 'It's OK, David,' I told myself. But I couldn't be soothed.

■

I found strength, as I had before, through soccer. I told myself that the way to get through this was to keep busy. Archangelo knew how much I loved soccer. He offered to take me to play with some other Sudanese guys on Saturday. I was new to Melbourne, so word of my arrival hadn't yet got around.

My cousin was very generous. He bought me some very cool Puma boots and soccer gear. He drove me to meet the other guys in Maidstone, in Melbourne's western suburbs. I walked in and was greeted by young men I hadn't seen since we had kicked around a soccer ball as teenagers in Kakuma.

There in front of me were Taban, Beny and Nhial. Their names had appeared on the Kakuma camp pinboard long before mine. Now here they were, looking healthy and happy. My loneliness and despair at the camp had started when these guys began to leave. And now we were together again.

Jamila's cousin was there, too. We knew each other from Kakuma. He had been close to Jamila and knew that I had been her boyfriend. I wanted to ask him about her but I couldn't. In our culture, you couldn't talk about these things. It would have brought her shame had I mentioned it.

They called themselves the Western Tigers, and the team included other Sudanese boys that I didn't know. After that first time I met them every weekend and, while we'd been serious about soccer in Kakuma, here we played for fun. I asked the boys why they weren't in a real competition with white people. They said it was too hard to find the time when you're working or studying full time.

Since Noriaki died, I had given up on my dream to be a professional footballer. I had the opportunity to briefly train with the Bulleen Zebras in the Victorian Premier League. My cousin had a friend who knew someone at the club, and linked me up. The coach told me I was good. My cousin drove me to a couple of training sessions. But I struggled to get there after that. I couldn't navigate the transport system to get to training, and it would have required going at least a couple of times a week. I didn't want to be a burden to Archangelo either, when he had already done so much for me. Plus I had bigger things to think about—whether I should go into full-time work or go to university. So I stopped training with the Bulleen Zebras and focused on playing with my friends.

My problems had become a lot smaller. In Africa, I was making daily decisions about life and death; how to eat, how not to get killed. Here, my First World problems were less critical. I never thought I'd be in a position where I would have choices, and I was struggling with it. In Africa, there were no choices; you did what you had to do to survive.

■

I went to see Sara the social worker, hoping she'd help with some answers. She told me that whether I chose work or study, she'd be able to help.

I thought my best opportunity was to go to a proper school. The problem was I had no idea what level I was at. I had finished high school in Kakuma, but I didn't know what the standard was like compared to Australia.

Sara told me all of my options: short courses, TAFE and university. After seeing some of my writing, she told me that she thought I was capable of going straight to university. I felt it was a special compliment coming from her.

She suggested that I also apply for a scholarship. I applied for various courses at Melbourne University and RMIT, including pathology and arts. I was keen on journalism and law, but I didn't have enough confidence in my English and knew you had to get really high marks to get into those courses.

My application was to commence university in 2005. I still had a few months to play with. I thought it would be good to get a job before I started university. Archangelo told me that there was a charity called the Brotherhood of St Laurence that could help me to find a job.

I wasn't fussy. I just wanted to work. I was blown away by the generosity in Australia, and I wanted to do something useful. But I had no idea what I could do. My cousin said that in this country there was work for everyone, regardless of your level of education.

As I walked to the Brotherhood of St Laurence, I practised saying in my head: 'Hello, will you be able to help me find a job?'

I walked into the building and approached the lady sitting at the reception desk. 'Please will you find me a job?' I blurted. She smiled, took my details and said someone would call me.

I waited for a few days, my anxiety growing. Then the phone call came.

Armed with an appointment, I returned. I met with a woman who asked me the funniest question ever directed at me. 'David, have you ever worked before?'

I just looked at her. Was she for real? I had assumed she knew where I came from. Didn't she know that refugees didn't work?

'I've never worked before,' I said. 'I've never been presented with that opportunity. This is the first interview I've had to get a job. Will you be able to find me a job?'

She laughed and said she would try. First, she wanted to know what skills I had.

'Everything, ma'am,' I said. 'I'm not fussy. I'm happy to clean toilets.'

'No problem,' she said. 'First, we will have to prepare a resumé. Have you heard of a resumé?'

'Yes, but I've never seen one,' I said. I began to worry that no employer would pick me. Why would they, when I had never had a job?

She said we'd look at it in a different way, by telling employers what I was good at. Good communication skills, the ability to learn quickly, that kind of thing. She told me she'd try a few companies, and she'd call me when she found something. Then she introduced me to a man named Paul.

'Welcome to Australia,' he said. 'We'll try our best to help.'

I waited for a couple of days. In my head, I was already spending the money I hadn't yet earned. I would buy sneakers and clothes and all the things I'd never had in Kakuma. Eventually, I'd buy a car.

With my Centrelink money, I bought my first mobile phone. I went back to the Brotherhood and gave them my phone number. The next day they called back and said they had a few options for jobs for me. The first job they wanted me to try was at Officeworks, a place that sells lots of stationery. My job would be stocking shelves. But first, I had to pass a computer test.

I'd never get the job now, I thought. I didn't know how to use a computer. Paul said not to worry. He'd teach me. My cousin let me play with his computer, too. I spent a night clicking things on the internet until I felt comfortable using it.

The following week Paul called me and told me there was a small piece of work at the Brotherhood, and did I want to do it? 'I'm free right now,' I said, setting off for the office immediately.

Paul had a pile of letters and wanted me to fold them and place them in envelopes, so that the address on the letter could be seen through the clear part of the envelope. He showed me how to fold the letters correctly.

I did almost 200 letters that day, and thoroughly enjoyed myself. I felt that I was doing something useful. Paul came back to check on me, praising my work. People walked past the office and stopped and said hello, and I had a cup of tea as I worked. It felt good.

Paul told me to come back the next day. There would be a few more letters, and then they'd pay me. I had assumed that I was just helping them out, because Paul was helping me. But the following day, after I did the remaining letters, Paul handed me an envelope with some money. It was the first time I had been paid to work.

'Do you want me to do some more?' I asked keenly.

Paul laughed and told me he'd call if there was any more work. I went home and showed my cousin the money. We spent it on meat and some other food.

■

Paul took me to Officeworks the next day. He introduced me to the manager, Michael, a friendly man who immediately made me feel at ease. He showed me around the big store. Then he took me to the computer for my test.

I passed. Michael congratulated me and told me to come back the next day to be measured for my uniform.

I was so excited. I rang Archangelo and told him I'd got the job. He was proud of me, and told me to tell Centrelink so they would stop giving me money.

Then I went to the Brotherhood and barged into Paul's office, interrupting a meeting. I still hadn't worked out that you weren't supposed to barge in on people's meetings. Paul laughed at the interruption. I told him my news and he said he'd call me later. I also told Father Patrick, with whom I'd become quite close.

So I began my life as an employed person. My job was to mainly stock shelves. Michael told me the key to the job was memory. You had to cram the location of all the stock into your brain. So when a customer asked for something they wanted, you could tell them what the store had.

Is that all? I thought. Cramming was something I excelled at. It was the way I had started to learn, before we had exercise books in Kakuma, and we'd done all our writing sitting beneath a tree, running a finger through the dirt.

My confidence grew as I found that I was quite good at my job. Customers would approach me and ask me for assistance in finding things. I loved that part of the job. I loved interacting with people, and being able to help.

I was so proud when I was paid for the first time. I gave some money to Archangelo and then took myself shopping. I bought some sneakers, a watch, some T-shirts. And for the first time, I sent some money to my friends in Kakuma. I came home with full arms and a contented heart.

It had taken more than twenty years, but the second Sudanese civil war was declared officially over in January 2005. The government of Sudan and the Sudan People's Liberation Army signed the Comprehensive Peace Agreement and many hoped that the deal would pave the way for greater autonomy in the south and, eventually, self-determination.

Under the agreement, the people of Southern Sudan would decide at a referendum in six years' time whether they wanted to be independent or remain part of Sudan. Until then, the south would effectively govern its own region. A Government of National Unity was formed, comprising members from the north and the south.

Omar al-Bashir remained president, while John Garang de Mabior became first vice president of this government, and president of Southern Sudan. But in July he died in a helicopter crash and was replaced by Salva Kiir, another senior member of the SPLA and a Dinka strongly in favour of secession from Sudan.

The peace deal did nothing to end the crisis still blazing in Darfur.

14

These White People Are Strange

I was stunned when the letter arrived. Not only had I been accepted into the pathology course at RMIT, but also into arts at Melbourne University.

Then came another surprising letter. Melbourne University wanted to give me a scholarship. So in 2005, at the age of twenty-seven, I would become an arts student at Melbourne University.

My excitement mingled with self-doubt. I had never dreamed that I'd go from writing with my finger in the dirt to attending a real university. My experiences had left me with very poor self-esteem when it came to learning. Even though I had completed high school in Kakuma, I was certain that the standard of education in the camp was much lower than it was in Australia.

I tried to imagine myself going to class with intelligent white people. I considered doing another course to prepare myself. But Sara and Archangelo encouraged me. They said I was smart and hard-working and I could do it.

I had been working at Officeworks for a few months and really enjoyed it. The people there had been really good to me. But I knew that if I was to succeed at university, I needed to concentrate on it full-time. So I left my job.

There was a ceremony at Melbourne University for those of us who'd been awarded scholarships. As I was shown to my seat I was asked, 'Are you here with your parents?'

'No, I'm here by myself,' I said, taken aback. As I took my seat on my own, I couldn't help but notice all the other students were sitting beside their parents. I was struck by a profound sadness as I watched the others smile and pose for photos with their families. I had missed out on being part of a family. And now, I felt the loss of my parents deeply.

The war in Sudan had just been declared officially over, and it made me wonder again whether my parents were alive. The war had smashed my family apart, and I had not seen my mother in almost twenty years.

■

I threw myself into my life as a student. I chose majors in politics and criminology. I thought about what had gone wrong in Sudan, and it seemed to me at least partly due to poor governance and a lack of democracy.

Father Patrick was a great help, paying for some of my books and other fees. I was all set. A week before I was due to start, I walked to the university to see how long it would take me to get there, so I wouldn't be late. I wandered around the campus, working out where all my classes were located. My prep work did little to relieve my anxiety.

I was a nervous wreck the night before classes started. Would I be the only black person? If I was, how would people treat me? Would I make friends? Should I talk to people? If I'm the only black person, I thought, all the focus will be on me and if I put my hand up to answer a question, I'd better give the correct answer.

What frightened me most was how I would be ranked in the class. I remembered that in Kakuma, students were ranked publicly and you would be shamed if you did badly. I imagined that it would be the same here. Surely I'd be at the bottom of the class. I couldn't bear the humiliation.

I built the situation up and up in my head. Before leaving home, I prayed and thanked God for the opportunity.

I dressed in jeans and a T-shirt, trying to look as Australian as possible. I wanted to blend in. I wanted to be as invisible as I had been when I was eight years old and Baba had told me to hide in the bushes as we fled Wau.

I walked from my Fitzroy flat to the university. I imagined that my class would have about fifty people. I entered the lecture theatre and was stunned. Was this a concert hall? We had had classes with eighty people in Kakuma, but this room could hold hundreds. Surely it wouldn't be full?

I was forty-five minutes early and the only person in the room. I couldn't work out where to sit. I walked to the back and sat in the last row. It didn't feel right. So I got up and took another seat in the middle. Still not right. As I continued to fret over where to sit, people began walking into the class. I wondered if anyone would sit beside me. They were talking easily to each other, sharing stories, and it felt like they already knew each other. No-one talked to me. Panicking, I finally moved to a seat three rows from the front. There was no way I'd be able to hear from the back.

I sat and waited. I noticed there was no blackboard. That was strange. How could the teacher teach without a blackboard? Instead, we were facing a big blank wall.

I took out my books and placed them on my lap. I was sitting in the centre of the row. As others came in and took their seats, all my fears were confirmed. No-one sat beside me. I wouldn't fit in. Maybe I should just get out now, I thought. I don't belong here.

To my amazement the room was quickly filling with people and noise. I looked around, searching for another black face, but couldn't see one.

The seats either side of me remained vacant. There were people sitting a few seats away talking to each other, ignoring me. People were sitting all around me but I might as well have been sitting alone.

Others were pulling out things from the side of their chairs and I realised they were desks. I tried to discreetly copy them, glancing around sheepishly, trying not to make a fool of myself. It took a while but I persisted, finally pulling out the desk, removing my books from my lap and putting them on the desk.

As the debate about whether I should stay continued in my head, the lecturer walked in. But no-one stood for him. I thought that was strange. In Africa, when a teacher walked into a room, everyone went silent and respectfully stood up until the teacher told you to take a seat.

I waited for a blackboard to appear but it didn't. People continued talking. Some were openly texting with their phones. Others walked into the room late. My mind was racing. Why wasn't the teacher doing anything to discipline these people who were misbehaving?

And then the lecturer tapped something and I could hear crackling sounds, and I worked out it was a microphone as he began speaking. I wondered how I was supposed to take notes when there was no blackboard. He was putting slides on a projector and moving through them rapidly and I had no time to write anything down. I looked around the room and people were scribbling furiously and I waited for him to write something, maybe on the wall, so I could start taking notes. I could not understand a thing and I hadn't written a word. The next thing I knew he was saying, 'See you next time.' Everyone began talking and leaving the room.

I sat frozen in shock. All my fears had been confirmed. Why was I doing this to myself? I could just get a job and make money immediately, without putting myself through this. I walked back to my flat in a state of high anxiety. I resolved to go to my next class in a few hours and if it was just as bad, I'd drop out.

It was. My frustration grew as it felt as though everyone was speaking three times more quickly than usual. The next class passed in a blur and I despondently walked home. I had managed to get through a whole day without understanding a single thing. Who was I kidding? I wasn't clever enough to go to university.

I went back the next day for my first tutorial class. I was relieved to find a much smaller class of about twelve people. A girl sat beside me and introduced herself. She asked me where I was from and I told her I was a refugee.

'Wow, you must be very clever!' she replied, and immediately my confidence lifted. We chatted for a while and when the teacher walked in I felt so much better for having had a conversation with someone.

The classroom had a whiteboard and the teacher was writing on it with a marker. That immediately made more sense to me. The whiteboard must be a relative of the blackboard. Things were looking up.

The tutor told us that to pass the subject, we had to attend ninety per cent of the classes. I was shocked that I would get marks simply for turning up. Why were they giving marks away for free? These white people were strange.

The other strange thing was that no-one raised their hands in this class. People talked when they had something to say. It was more like an informal discussion. I was more familiar with not being allowed to speak unless you raised your hand. I took down notes as the debate went on around me. By the end of the class I was the only person who hadn't said anything. The tutor asked me if I had anything to contribute. Intimidated, I replied, 'No, I have nothing else to add.'

I wanted to explain to him why. So as the others left the room, I stayed back. I told the tutor that I was from Africa, and this was all new to me. I told him about my education in Kakuma. He responded kindly and told me that in this class, there was no right or wrong. But I thought that was impossible. I had been taught that one plus one equalled two and there was no argument. I had been taught to think only about facts. There had been no free discussion of ideas where I came from.

The following week the tutor gave me a tip that was like gold to me: every lecture was recorded and you could listen to it online as many times as you wanted to. All you had to do was log in with your student number. I beamed with relief.

Still, even though I could now replay the lectures multiple times and take notes, university remained a hard slog for me. I had to read everything three times to understand it. And I had to do so much more work to feel that I was even close to the same level as the other students.

Eventually I settled down and even began to enjoy myself a little. I especially liked the political subjects. I learnt about democracy, and European studies, and the history of the Cold War, and different political ideologies.

I buried myself in study as my internal struggle persisted. I had been in Australia for a few months, but had done nothing about my lingering trauma. I ruled out seeing a counsellor. I didn't think there was anything new that anyone could tell me. I thought that only someone who had been through what I had been through could help me.

I also avoided watching the international news. I couldn't bear the stories of famine and disease and war. It pushed me to the brink and the memories came flooding back.

One day, by sheer coincidence, I came face to face with a good memory. I was at Footscray train station and bumped into Lueth. I didn't even know he'd come to Australia, as we'd never had the chance to say goodbye to each other in Kakuma. I was so happy to see him and as we embraced, he told me he was now a soccer referee. He asked me if I was still playing soccer and I told him that I was playing for fun. We swapped details and vowed to stay in touch.

I was reminded again of my parents, and wondered whether they were alive. I was desperate for closure. I thought that maybe Baba had made it. But I had little hope that Mama had survived the war. I spent a lot of time praying for them with Father Patrick.

But I kept my suffering to myself. I concocted a system where one part of me was in deep pain, and another part of me went into comfort mode. I soothed myself with the thought that I had left that terrible place and I was safe. I began to question myself. I wasn't just a victim of a war. Perhaps I had played a role in it. We all had. We were instruments used by politicians for their own agenda. Then I wondered what I could do about it, but couldn't find any answers.

I began skipping lectures when I knew there would be discussions about war. The peace agreement in Sudan had just been signed, but I had my doubts. I wondered how this agreement would be any different to previous broken deals.

The war in Iraq particularly got to me. In my mind, the US-led invasion of Iraq, just like the war in Sudan, was in part linked to oil. I was so angry at Australia's involvement.

So when a rally protesting the Iraq war was organised, I felt I had to go. I was burning with anger the whole time. I wanted to grab the microphone and scream into it: 'This is not what we should be doing!'

After the rally I wandered into a park, sat beneath a tree, and couldn't stop the tears.

■

I looked forward to soccer every weekend. When I played soccer, there were no thoughts of war in my head. My mind was blank.

I was one of the senior players and enjoyed helping the less experienced boys. I'd always volunteer to stay behind and show the boys some skills. We had lots of friendly matches with other Sudanese teams from the south-east and the Sunshine area. They were teams in the same position as ours—they wanted to play but weren't part of an official competition. Often we'd pitch in some money and have a barbecue after the game. We all looked forward to Saturdays, when we'd catch up with our friends and play soccer.

We had a team manager, Michael, a Sudanese man who had been one of the first to come to Australia. Our team was very inclusive, and open to any Sudanese young person who wanted to play.

We longed to play in a real competition. Our greatest problem, though, was that the pitch in Maidstone where we usually played didn't belong to us. Without a home ground, we couldn't join a competition. Sometimes, the club that owned the field where we trained would turn up while we were playing and we'd have to leave.

We put in some requests to a couple of the local councils to help us find a place to train, but nothing happened. So we continued moving between pitches, playing wherever we could, just for the love of the game.

Sometimes we'd turn up to a field and there'd already be a game underway. We'd sit and watch the game and wait our turn.

We played the odd friendly with a team from the Sunshine police. Of course, our boys were more skilled than the police team, but it was a good opportunity to interact with each other.

I was playing soccer with Jamila's cousin, but as the months went on I still hadn't talked to him about her. She was living in another country and I hadn't forgotten her, even as I had adapted to my new life in Australia. One day, he brought it up.

'Jamila is doing really well at uni,' he said unexpectedly.

'That's really nice,' I replied, grateful for the chance to talk about her.

He must have figured out that I wanted to get in touch with her. He turned up to soccer one day and told me he had spoken to Jamila, and gave me her email address. I eagerly wrote to her, telling her I was glad she was safe, and giving her my phone number.

She emailed back that she was glad I had made it to Australia, and asked me if I was at university. Education had always been very important to her.

Then she called me, and I knew my feelings for her hadn't changed. I told her I still loved her and wanted to marry her. I had never hidden my love for her, not even when I had been a player, dating other girls at the same time.

After that first call, we talked often. She encouraged me to continue focusing on study. She thought I had the potential to achieve great things.

My days as a player (with women) were over. I wanted only Jamila. I began fantasising about marrying her. I wanted to find my parents first, to gain their blessing. We were in love, and I was so excited about my future with her.

We talked regularly, making plans to be together again.

■

I struggled all through my first year of university and failed one subject—creative writing. I juggled trying to get to know people and learning how to get around the university's vast campus, and also just settling into my new country while still dealing with my lingering trauma.

So many times I came close to quitting. I'd be sitting in class feeling overwhelmed and foolish because I couldn't contribute. I lacked so much knowledge about Australian politics, knowledge that the other students had acquired from growing up in this country.

I completed my first year of university unsure that I would continue. I felt as though I had done three times more work than everyone else. I was so exhausted from repeatedly listening to lectures online until I understood them, and from staying up all night studying. There was little time for socialising, and I struggled to make friends. The whole experience was quite lonely for me.

It was particularly hard when I noticed other Sudanese people who had never gone to university were driving around in big cars. I had always thought that the only way to make money was through education. But it was different in Australia. My friends were working in factories and making enough money to buy cars. I kept questioning why I was putting so much pressure on myself when I could make money immediately. Still, I felt that I owed it to myself to finish university. It was an opportunity I'd never thought I would have.

At least other students were sitting beside me in class now. I slowly felt as though I was blending in among the sea of white faces. I even spotted some other black people on campus.

My thoughts never strayed far from my friends suffering in Kakuma. I thought of them still surviving on rations. I made a point of saving my Centrelink money and sending some back to them, even if it meant going without lunch some days. We had grown up taking care of each other, and being apart wouldn't change that.

The crisis in Darfur claimed more lives amid accusations of genocide, and the exodus from Darfur to refugee camps in Chad continued. There were more than 200 000 refugees from Sudan seeking help in Chad in 2006, according to the UNHCR Global Report. However, it said, the humanitarian and civilian character of the camps was violated by Sudanese rebel groups who recruited refugee children in and around the camps.

With the peace deal between the government of Sudan and the Sudan People's Liberation Army signed, Sudanese from the south could start to return home. The UNHCR reported that it facilitated the repatriation of some 26 000 Sudanese refugees to Southern Sudan in 2006. But about 73 000 Sudanese refugees were in Kenyan camps that year, of whom almost half were children.

In a sign of the fragility of the peace deal, clashes erupted in the southern Sudanese town of Malakal at the end of 2006. It was the deadliest fighting between government forces and the SPLA since the peace deal had been signed.

15

Talking to the Enemy

Whenever I shut my eyes, it was like someone had pressed play on a violent movie. And I was the star.

I still couldn't sleep. I'd sit up all night watching television, willing myself to get sleepy. I became obsessed with keeping busy. Doing nothing frightened me, because it would give me time to think. And then the images would come rushing back.

I contemplated taking pills that would knock me out quickly. But I didn't want to get hooked on sleeping pills. I tried to train myself to sleep. I'd stay up late watching movies until my eyes drooped. Or I'd punish myself with a long, hard run until I was exhausted. But I woke easily. All it took was a footstep to rouse me. My soldier training had taught me to only ever half-sleep. And even now, I could not seek complete oblivion.

I felt like I was quietly having a meltdown. But I wouldn't talk about it, not even with my cousins. It was as though we had all made an unspoken pact not to verbalise what we had gone through. Occasionally we'd make jokes about it. I'd reminisce about how good I had been at stealing food. Laughing took the sting out of the horrendous stories. But I never talked about burying my friends. I wanted to lock that away.

I began my second year of university with my head still a mess. I decided that what I needed was to be inspired. I needed to know more about great people who had fought for justice and gone through great suffering. I began to read about Nelson Mandela and Mahatma Gandhi, drawing strength and comfort from their suffering and from what they had achieved.

I also thought I could distance myself from my own pain by helping others. Back in Africa, I had heard about an organisation called the National Council of Churches. I discovered there was one in Australia and went to see a man who worked there named Visier. He told me I could help by sharing my story. He put me in touch with the organisation Initiatives of Change, which ran a course called Life Matters.

The title of the course threw me. Does life really matter? I had come to believe that it didn't. I was going through the motions of survival while being tormented by images from my past. Death would have been a relief from the suffering. I still carried so much pain and hatred, a hatred that irrationally extended to all Muslim people. I was physically in Australia, but dying internally because of what was happening to my country and my family and friends in Africa.

It was a nine-day live-in course, and I agreed to do it during the university break. The course aimed to make you reflect on your past to help you move forward. There were people with all sorts of backgrounds. What we had in common was our traumatic pasts.

I found the whole thing very confronting. I sat listening to the others tell their stories, dreading having to speak. When it was my turn, I couldn't do it. I walked out of the session and sat in another room by myself, a mass of emotions mingling inside me.

Two men, Rob and John, later found me in that state. They told me that sharing my story would help me let go of the pain of the past, and give me the strength to move forward.

I locked myself alone in a room that night and cried for hours. I thought that to tell my story would be to relive it. But I also realised that I had been in Australia for two years. I couldn't go on like that.

The next day I told them I was ready. And for the first time, with voice composed, I told my entire story. The audience sat quietly and listened. By the time I finished speaking, some of them were crying.

To my surprise and relief, the heavy burden I had carried for twenty years felt instantly lighter. I began to look at things differently. I had found my turning point.

■

Jamila and I continued to talk regularly on the phone, making plans. One day, I got a phone call from her that changed everything. 'David, I don't think you will like to hear this,' she began.

I went dead on the other end of the phone as she told me that her parents had chosen a man for her to marry. She would be forced to marry a man she didn't love.

I knew that arranged marriages were still common in our culture, and you didn't defy your parents. But I couldn't say anything. I had waited years to marry Jamila. And now we would be forever separated by her parents.

We did consider defying them. We made plans. I'd work hard to raise the cash to go to her. We'd elope. Then we'd call her parents, who were still in Africa, and tell them what we had done. We'd force their hand. But I didn't want to come between her and her family. It would have been a scandal in our culture, and I did not want that for her. We'd never be forgiven. Nor could I afford the dowry. In our culture, an educated Sudanese woman living in a Western country is worth a large dowry of more than 100 cows. It would have cost thousands of dollars. I was a poor student. There's no way I could have raised that kind of money.

Talking to each other became too painful. We severed all communication. She went on to marry the man her parents had chosen, and I was heartbroken.

I permitted myself a tiny piece of hope. I imagined that one day, even if she had children, she'd break up with him. And I'd be waiting for her.

■

Now that I had shared my story, I realised that I could use it for good. I turned my attention to thinking about positive solutions for the trouble that persisted in Sudan. And I thought the key was forgiveness.

I had allowed my hatred for the northern Sudanese to fester for years. I had packed the hatred in my bag and brought it to Australia with me. But now I wanted to let it go. I didn't want my children to inherit my hatred.

The way I saw it now, the war had taken sons and daughters from both the north and the south. I wanted to forgive the people of the north for all the pain they had caused us. But I also wanted to forgive the people of the south, and even myself for the role I may have unwittingly played.

I began searching for people from northern Sudan living in Australia. Through a friend I was given the details of a woman named Faten.

I made the phone call. 'Hello,' I said. 'I'm from Southern Sudan. You don't know me but I'm calling because I want to have a chat to you about our country.'

There was surprised silence. Then: 'No problem.'

We organised a time to meet. I introduced myself and told her, 'I want to forgive all the people from the north for what happened. And I hope you have other contacts that I can talk to, particularly young people.'

Then I told her my story. By now, I could tell it fluently. She cried as I told her everything. Then she said: 'David, on behalf of my people, I honestly beg for forgiveness. You shouldn't have gone through that.'

I told her that this was the beginning of a new journey, that the root of our problems in Sudan could be religion or resources or something else. But as young people, we needed to look at it differently. I told her that if the north and the south didn't work together, the war would continue to be fought by every generation that came after us. It was our responsibility to end the cycle of violence.

She wanted to help. Together, we started a group called Sudanese Youth for Reconciliation and Hope with some other people—Biong, Ola, Akec, Tashir and Ahmed. We thought we could bring people from the north and the south together peacefully, by sharing our stories.

We organised a meeting. Initiatives of Change allowed us to use a room at their centre for free, and it was on. I told my cousins of our plan and they were supportive. But it was harder to persuade others from the south who thought I was crazy to speak to—let alone for-give—the people who were meant to be our enemies.

I woke the morning of our meeting feeling anxious. I desperately wanted this to work. I envisaged that our small gathering could be the starting point for solving the bigger picture of war plaguing our country. I had put out the word and left it up to people to decide if they wanted to come. Many friends told me it was too soon, that they needed more time to heal. I would have been happy if two or three people showed up. In the end, about thirty did, almost evenly divided between the north and the south.

It was shocking and awkward at first. I think we were afraid of each other, afraid of what might happen, afraid of the hatred taking over. I was the first to stand and speak. I shared my story again. It was getting easier to tell it. I told the room that every Southern Sudanese person had their own painful story. I was choosing to share mine to demonstrate what we had gone through, both as a nation and as individuals.

I told them we should clear our hearts and move forward together. And then I said something controversial: 'Anyone from the north here today, I forgive you.'

My words did not go down well with some of my friends. They still weren't ready to forgive.

Faten is a young woman who is both brilliant and brave. She stood and begged for forgiveness on behalf of her people. I think her speech had greater impact than mine. The room fell silent as she spoke with sincere passion. And then others began to speak up, and tell their own stories.

Then we shared a meal together. It was the first time I'd shared a meal with the people I had been taught to hate and kill.

The day had been so successful that we decided to meet regularly. But it pissed off a lot of people. Soon, the phone calls came from as far as Adelaide and Sydney, from people who had heard of what

I was doing. They were people who wanted the hatred for the north to persist. 'David, how dare you do this?' they demanded. 'They are our enemy and we should be thinking of ways to destroy them!'

I tried to explain what I was doing. I asked them if they wanted the cycle of hate to be passed on to their children. I asked them if they wanted the war to continue forever.

But there was no reasoning with some people. Ugly accusations emerged. They said I was being bribed by the north. I refused to allow the negativity to stop me. I knew that Faten and I had started something important. Even though the peace agreement had been signed in Sudan a year earlier, our country still wasn't really at peace.

I thought if the people of the north and south got to know each other, it would be harder for them to kill. Because the enemy would no longer be faceless.

■

As my work in the Sudanese community gained a higher profile, more opportunities came. I liked working with young people. I felt that change started with the younger generations.

Then I got a call from a woman named Kate, who worked at the Brotherhood of St Laurence. The organisation ran a 'breakfast club' program for children, mostly those from Vietnam and Sudan. They wanted to get someone with a Sudanese background to be a role model for the kids. They had heard about the good work I was doing and were keen for me to volunteer one morning a week.

When I checked out the program, I fell in love with it immediately. And the hours worked well with my classes at university. I spent the morning playing with the kids, some of whom were living in the same housing commission flats where I lived.

The breakfast club began when it emerged that many struggling families in the area were sending their children to school without breakfast. By mid-morning, some of the children were unable to concentrate and were dozing off in class. Eating a healthy breakfast was a good way to improve their performance in the classroom. The kids were given a nutritious meal of cereal, fruit and toast. Then there were activities.

I was really moved by the program, partly because I could relate to these kids. Where I came from, breakfast was unthinkable. But that was Africa. I was outraged that in a wealthy country like Australia there were families who couldn't afford to feed their children breakfast.

The great irony of my latest project dawned on me—I had never eaten breakfast, and here I was working for a program whose main purpose was to feed breakfast to children who otherwise would go without it. So on the mornings I volunteered, I'd leave home without eating breakfast, and then proceed to explain to the children how crucial it was to eat breakfast. 'Why don't you eat?' they'd ask. I'd tell them that I'd already eaten at home.

I'd grown up with the mindset that food was so precious that you'd eat only if you were hungry. And I'm never hungry in the morning.

■

I threw myself into my work in the Sudanese community. The Initiatives of Change continued to let us use their resources and I moved into its community house in Toorak, sharing it with others. I told my cousins that what Faten and I had started was a big deal and I wanted to be around people who would encourage me and help build my faith.

It was the first time I had shared a home with white people. I had my own room and we shared a bathroom and kitchen. We shared meals, and I even learned to like broccoli.

It was a challenging time while I juggled so much. I was still at university but I retreated slightly from soccer because I was so passionate about what Faten and I were doing.

We helped to organise the first Sudanese–Australian youth conference, and it was a great success. Soon I felt brave enough to initiate contact with politicians in the north and south of Sudan. I wanted them to talk to each other, and to start a process of national reconciliation. That, I thought, would help the whole nation to heal.

Through my contacts, I was connected with politicians on both sides and began writing to them. I also wrote of my idea to Riek Machar, who had become vice president of Southern Sudan after the peace deal was signed.

We raised some money and sent a delegation to the north and south of Sudan. Faten, Biong and Akec were among the group. They talked to politicians and to young people about the need to launch a process of reconciliation.

Meanwhile, I was still getting angry emails and phone calls from people who insisted that I was being bribed by the north. I could understand their suspicion; they thought that while those from the south were dreaming of autonomy, the north were doing all they could to remain one country.

I made it clear that I wanted South Sudan's independence as much as they did.

Preparations to help the Southern Sudanese refugees go home were well underway. According to the UNHCR Global Report 2007, plans were made that year for the voluntary repatriation of more than 100 000 refugees who had been living in the Central African Republic, the Democratic Republic of the Congo, Egypt, Ethiopia, Kenya and Uganda. It said that some 70 000 returned to their war-ravaged homes.

While the world's attention remained locked on the continuing crisis in Darfur, Sudan's Comprehensive Peace Agreement between the north and the south was in danger of collapsing. The Sudan People's Liberation Movement briefly suspended its participation in the government of National Unity, accusing the north of failing to abide by the peace agreement. But after more discussions between the two parties, it returned to the government by the end of 2007.

16

Losing My Mother's Tongue

After the peace deal was signed, some people felt it was safe enough to return to Southern Sudan to visit their families, who had defied the terror of the war and stayed. That's how I learnt that my father was alive.

It was 2007, and a friend from Kakuma now living in Canada came to visit us in Melbourne. We had a gathering to welcome him. He told me that he had recently been in Southern Sudan, and had seen my father in Turalei. My father didn't have a phone. But my friend gave me the phone number of a man nearby who had a satellite phone.

I phoned the man and told him I was looking for my father, Vincent Mangok Ayuel. The man knew him, but he wasn't in Turalei. 'Call back in three days,' he said. 'I'll be back in Turalei, and I'll connect you.'

I thanked God that my father was alive. I hadn't seen him since he had left Kakuma. I hoped he had found my mother, and they were both safe. Three days later, I called back. The man had kept his promise. He said to call back in an hour and he'd be with my father.

When I called again, my father answered the phone. 'Baba, are you OK?' I asked. And then, 'Where's Mama?'

He didn't know where she was. He had tried to find her. But when he had left Kakuma and returned to Wau, she wasn't there, and the house had been destroyed. The sight of the charred house must have made him conclude that she was dead.

But he had found Abuk. She was the first person he had located when he returned to Sudan. She had stayed in Turalei the whole time, and married a man who had known my father and me in Pinyudo. Baba had been his teacher in the camp. The man she married hadn't come to Kenya with us; after we fled Ethiopia he had gone to war and survived. When the war was over, he had returned to the village and met Abuk. He had made her laugh with stories of my cheekiness in the camp. After they married, she had moved away to her husband's village. I couldn't talk to her, because she was too far from Turalei.

He asked if I was OK. I told him I really wanted to find Mama.

Baba had been pressured by his relatives into remarrying, and he had had more children. Initially he had tried to resist, telling them that he didn't want to marry unless he knew for sure my mother was dead.

Our conversation was long and unemotional. We spoke in Dinka. I had picked up my father's language while in the camps with all the other Dinka boys, and could speak it fluently now.

We talked until the credit on my phone ran out, and resolved that we wouldn't lose touch again. Speaking to Baba had provided some relief. But I couldn't stop worrying about Mama. I was almost resigned to the fact that she was dead.

■

My father and I remained in regular contact. I told him of the work I was doing and he was pleased. He said it was something Sudan needed, and he hoped people would hear me out.

In July 2007, I was invited to attend a conference in Switzerland bringing together people who had experienced war. Initiatives of Change raised the money to send me. Others from the north and the south of Sudan were also attending, including Southern Sudanese vice president Riek Machar. I hoped I would have the chance to meet him.

I flew into Geneva and got the train to a small town called Caux, where the conference was being held.

Someone had told Riek Machar about me, and I was invited to have breakfast with him and some delegates from Southern Sudan. I told him my story, and of the work I was doing in Australia. He told me to make use of the opportunities that I had and to study hard, because Southern Sudan would need my skills if I went back. They were encouraging words from a man I saw as a leader.

The following day, I shared my story at the conference. My audience listened in moved silence. They told me that what had happened to me should never happen again to anyone.

A woman who was a Sudanese member of parliament approached me after my speech, and we sat down and had a chat. 'I'm from Wau, too,' she said. 'What's your mother's tribe?'

I told her my mother was from the Bai tribe.

She looked thoughtfully at me. Then she asked my mother's name. I told her.

She gasped and stood up and began pacing. I froze as I watched her agitated movements. Clearly, this woman knew my mother. I braced myself for the bad news. Then she sat beside me and hugged me tearfully.

'David, I know your mother!' she said. 'I know where she is!'

I didn't dare believe her. Surely it wasn't possible to find a connection to my mother in Switzerland, of all the places in the world! I listened in quiet shock as she said that after the war had swept through Wau, Mama and my sisters had fled to another village. She had last seen Mama there about a year ago. And she believed that Mama was still there.

I worried that she was mistaken. Maybe she was talking about another woman named Tereza. But if it was the same person, it meant that Mama had been alive as recently as a year ago. I didn't wait until I got home. I phoned Baba from the conference and repeated the woman's story, and told him I was sending him money to help him find Mama.

I went back to my room still stunned, sat on the bed, and let myself cry for the woman who had been robbed of the right to be my mother. Then I prayed.

■

A couple of weeks after I returned to Australia, I phoned my father. The first words he uttered were words I never thought I would hear: he had found Mama.

She was in the village, where the woman had said she would be, living in an overcrowded hut with my elder sisters and some other people that my father and I didn't know. Baba had moved them all back to Wau, where they were now staying in another overcrowded hut, and he had returned to Turalei.

I thanked God that she was alive. But I couldn't bring myself to feel anything else.

A few weeks later, when Baba was in Wau, I called them. I spoke to Baba first, then to a woman whose voice I didn't recognise.

'Hello Mama,' I said in broken Arabic. She responded in rapid Bai—the language she thought that I knew.

She continued speaking into the phone, and I quickly came to the distressing realisation that I couldn't understand her. I had forgotten my mother's tongue. Years of being around Dinka boys in the camps meant that I had adopted that language fluently, but had forgotten the languages I had learnt as a child—Arabic and Bai.

I tried to speak to her in my very broken Arabic, but it was no use—we couldn't understand each other. I felt totally disconnected to this woman who was my mother. I hadn't missed her, but I had missed the idea of her, and the idea of belonging to a family. Maybe if I had lived among other women I could have missed her. But I had grown up around men and boys, with nothing resembling a maternal touch.

I've never told my parents I love them. It's what happens when you're embroiled in war. You develop other relationships that become more valuable than the one you should have had with your parents.

Our frustrating exchange was brief. Mama put my father back on the phone, and he told me that they were all OK. But I learned, too, of the impoverished conditions in which they were all living. I listened sadly as he told me of their dire situation with food. Nothing had changed since I had left as a little boy. My family was still barely surviving on one meal a day.

∎

I kept hearing from my friends about this guy named Emmanuel. Apparently he was a Sudanese singer based in Britain, and he was really cool. It never occurred to me that he was the friend that I had assumed had been killed with so many others that dreadful day we'd fled the Ethiopian guns while trying to cross the Gilo River.

But people who had known both of us in Pinyudo insisted that my friend Emmanuel was alive and had become a big star. I brushed it off. I had locked memories of Emmanuel away. He had been part of my crew. Together, we had found ways to escape the hell of our existence by climbing the mango trees and running amok. And now I feared that revisiting those childhood memories and making inquiries about him would only confirm his death.

I didn't take it any further until I was part of the organising committee of a youth conference. We wanted someone of significance to attend. Someone suggested I contact the singer Emmanuel Jal, because apparently we had been friends so many years ago.

I googled him and found lots of photos of a man who bore a striking resemblance to my childhood friend. It struck me that maybe it was him. I wasn't keen on Facebook, but it was the only way I could think of to get in touch with him. So I joined Facebook and, even though I didn't have a profile picture, I sent him a friend request.

He quickly accepted. Maybe he thought I was one of his fans? So I sent him a private message. 'Hey, this is David Nyuol. Do you remember me?'

'Hey, is that the Nyuol I remember?' he wrote back.

I uploaded a photo of myself and replied: 'Yes.'

We exchanged more excited messages and swapped phone numbers. Then I got a call one night that immediately took me back several years. 'Dude! You're still surviving!' he exclaimed.

'Yeah, I'm still surviving, man,' I replied, grinning. 'Emmanuel, is that you that I hear is singing?'

I couldn't get over the fact that my friend could sing!

'I'm glad I found you,' he said. 'Remember our days back in the camp? There was a film made about us!'

It hadn't clicked at the time, but while Emmanuel and I had been talking to the white people in Ethiopia, someone was making a film about us. I had thought they were just recording us as we talked about our lives.

But a filmmaker had archived the footage. When Emmanuel became big and began talking publicly about his history, the filmmaker wondered if he was one of the boys he had filmed years ago. He approached Emmanuel and showed him his footage, including the footage of Emmanuel and me. They went on to make a film called *War Child*.

It turned out that while I was fleeing Sudan and then living in Kakuma, Emmanuel had been a child soldier in Sudan. Then he was rescued by Emma McCune, a British aid worker who had been married to Riek Machar. She had smuggled Emmanuel into Kenya, and later adopted him and took care of him until she died in a car accident. He had ended up in the slums of Nairobi before going to Britain.

I was amazed at his story. Then we talked about what we had each been doing in the community. We realised that many years had gone by but we still had much in common—we both shared the desire for reconciliation in Sudan. He was already a big peace activist, and out there through his music about the suffering in Sudan. They were songs crying out for peace.

That first conversation went on for ages, as we laughed and talked shit and teased each other. It was like getting to know each other all over again. He wasn't able to make it to the conference—my original reason for getting in touch with him. But we resolved to collaborate on ideas on how we could bring peace to our country.

Reconnecting with my parents and Emmanuel got me thinking more about Sudan and filled me with a new resolve: it was time to go back.

So I deferred university and went to work full time in a furniture factory, sanding cupboards and chairs. I saved as much money as I could and sent it back to my parents, while continuing to send money to my friends in Kakuma. A few months later, I boarded a plane bound for Sudan.

Security in the south of Sudan remained tense, despite the signing of the peace deal. There were attacks by unknown gunmen in some areas. The UNHCR reported that it was forced to cancel a planned mission to Magwi in the Sudanese state of Eastern Equatoria because of a series of ambushes in which people were abducted and killed.

Refugees returned to Southern Sudan after years away, only to face a humanitarian crisis. The United Nations reported that between January and late April 2007, more than 630 people had died from meningitis and 340 from diarrhoea in Southern Sudan.

Tribal conflict also persisted in the south. The UN Office for the Coordination of Humanitarian Affairs reported in November 2007 that eight Dinka Bor had been killed and thousands of heads of cattle stolen during a cattle raid near Padak. Other Dinka Bor were later ambushed while attempting to recover the stolen cattle. The UNOCHA report said that 27 people were killed and 48 were wounded in the exchange of fire. Six of those killed were Murle and 21 Dinka Bor. In a 'revenge attack', the Dinka Bor stormed the Médecins Sans Frontières–run hospital in Bor and killed four Murle patients, the UNOCHA said. Three more Murle were killed in other parts of Bor.

17

An Alien in My Country

I never thought I'd willingly visit the home of my enemies. But there I was, on a plane headed for Khartoum in northern Sudan.

It had taken a long time to build up the courage to book my ticket and fly into a city full of people who had been taught to hate me. My own hatred for the northern Sudanese and Muslims was gone, superseded by the bigger picture. And that was a Sudan where the people of the north and south could live together peacefully.

Still, I was filled with anxiety and doubt about whether I should be doing this. I worried about what might happen to me when I arrived. I knew that going around Sudan advocating for reconciliation with the people who had been our enemies was not only highly controversial, but potentially dangerous. It was an idea that could cost me my life. I also worried that landing in Khartoum would bring back graphic memories that I was still fighting hard to suppress, and the hatred would come back. But at the same time, I felt mentally prepared; I had strengthened my mind before boarding the plane.

I was not yet an Australian citizen, so I didn't have a passport. But the Immigration Department had given me a document enabling me to travel. I had to apply for a visa to enter Sudan, as I had no proof that I was born there. I was somewhat bemused by the situation—I had spent years trying to escape Africa, only to have to obtain a visa now to enter my own country.

A friend knew someone in Khartoum who could help me get a visa. The visa was scanned and emailed to me, so it was printed on a separate piece of paper instead of attached to my travel document.

My flight would go via Bangkok and Dubai. I was all set. But on the day of my flight, I realised I had lost my visa. When I checked in at Melbourne Airport, a man from the airline told me I needed a visa. 'Are you from Sudan?' he asked. I told him I was. He said that it should be fine, and allowed me to board the flight.

I didn't think of my misplaced visa again, until I arrived in Bangkok. 'Sir, we can't allow you onto the plane without a visa,' I was told when I was about to board the plane.

I had lost my visa, I said, but I was from Sudan.

'Prove it,' was the unmoved reply. Of course I couldn't. It's not as though I could pull out my birth certificate, because I didn't have one.

My blood was boiling. I couldn't work out who I was angrier with—myself for losing the visa, or the airline. I had no choice but to stay in Bangkok while waiting for a letter to be emailed to me from Khartoum, confirming that I had been granted a visa to enter Sudan. It took three days.

I stayed in a cheap hotel while I waited, fuming the whole time at the absurd situation. I had been desperate to get out of Sudan, and now I was being made to jump through hoops to get back in.

I didn't leave my hotel the whole time I was in Bangkok, except to make phone calls and check the Internet. I was afraid of going out and getting lost. When the letter arrived I returned to the airport, fighting to curb my frustration at the delay, and boarded the flight to Dubai without incident.

It was on the last leg of my journey that I began to falter. As I drew closer to Khartoum, I began to question myself: Who was I to so easily let go of all my pain? Then the images rushed back to my head and tortured me once more, and I longed for something to knock me out so I could sleep. The images refused to leave for the entire journey to Khartoum.

■

A man was due to meet me at the airport, but we didn't know each other. I looked around the airport terminal, trying to spot a man who looked like he was waiting for me.

There were two queues—one for foreigners and one for nationals. Not for the first time, I felt like a stranger in my own country as I joined the white people in the foreigners' line.

A man in military garb pointed at the sign and barked at me in Arabic: 'Are you blind and stupid? You're in the wrong line!'

I couldn't read the signs in Arabic, but I could understand with my broken Arabic what the man was saying. I moved to the Sudanese queue without saying a word. I was soon approached by another military man. 'Are you dumb?' he shouted. 'Go to the other queue!'

I was getting angry, but I was determined not to lose my cool. I returned to the back of the foreigners' queue and waited. Then came military man number three, who tapped me on the shoulder and said more pleasantly, 'You're supposed to be in the Sudanese line.'

My frustration mounting, I resolved to wait until every passenger who had been on my flight had gone through immigration. If I was the last man, then someone would have to see me. I took a seat, swallowing back tears. This is my country, I thought, and I can't get in. Shouldn't I be welcomed back to Sudan, instead of being treated like an alien? Adding to my frustration was my inability to properly understand Arabic—the language I had spoken fluently as a child. I had barely made out the words of the military men.

As I sat and waited, I was approached by a man who had observed my movement between queues. 'Are you David?' he asked me in Dinka. 'I saw what happened.'

It was a man from Southern Sudan, the man who was meant to meet me. 'Wait here,' he said. It wasn't like I was going anywhere!

He returned a few minutes later with a tall Southern Sudanese man with big military stars on his uniform who said, 'Follow me.' He pushed past all the other passengers and took me to the front of the foreigners' queue. This was more like it. I felt sorry for the others who were waiting. But this was Africa; here, it was all about who you knew.

We got into a car and drove through the streets of Khartoum. It was hot and dusty and packed with people dressed in robes. They dressed differently to the way we did in the south. I kept thinking that these were the people who had put us through so much pain.

Car horns beeped incessantly around us as we drove to my hotel. Once in my room, I took out the phone numbers of the people I had planned to meet and called them one by one, organising meetings. I talked to women's groups. And I met university students who were from the north and south. We sat in a circle and, speaking in English, I shared my story. My words were well received and I was inspired by these young people who were looking forward to a different Sudan.

I was interviewed by the local newspapers and on the television about what I was doing in Sudan. I told them that my aim was to get both politicians and the people from the north and the south talking to each other about what had happened, so we could forgive one another. I thought that by talking to each other, we would build mutual respect as human beings and learn to peacefully co-exist— Muslims and Christians.

I wanted the government of Sudan—which included politicians from the south as well—to endorse and launch a process of national reconciliation. I wasn't the first to think of it, but I wanted to give this highly contentious idea a push. It could happen only if the politicians backed it with resources.

In hindsight, my approach with the politicians was all wrong. I should have told them what they needed to do. I had thought it would be enough to broach the idea with them, and then see what they did with it. The thing about politicians is they may give the impression that they're listening, but then you walk out of a meeting and nothing happens. And despite all the great discussions we had, nothing happened.

My trip to Khartoum and meetings with politicians had reignited the accusations that I was being bribed. I tried to respond with understanding. But I couldn't help but feel angry.

∎

There was a knock on the door of my hotel room. I opened the door to find a man I had known since I was a boy in Kakuma. It had been years since we had seen each other.

'Hey! How did you know I'm here?' I grinned as we hugged.

'I saw you around and followed you the other day,' he said.

We went to a cafe and had some tea and swapped stories. I offered to pay but he wouldn't let me. He had a car and offered to drive me around. I asked him what he was doing now. He was a security man based in Khartoum.

I was really happy to see him. As we drove around, I told him what I was doing in Sudan. I spoke passionately about wanting reconciliation. He seemed interested in what I had to say, and I thought I was winning him over.

The following day, I got a phone call from Riek Machar's wife Angelina Teny, now a minister in the government. She wanted me to see her. My friend drove me to our meeting.

She offered me tea in her nice office and we chatted. I found her very impressive and clever as I told her why I was in Sudan. She responded positively and offered to put me on a plane to meet her husband in Juba, the capital of Southern Sudan. I emerged from our meeting encouraged, and went to meet my friend for lunch. We were eating and chatting. And then he dropped a bombshell.

'David, I have known you since we were little,' he said soberly. 'I'm going to be honest with you. Three of us are on a rotational shift watching you.'

They had been sent from the south to spy on me. He wasn't supposed to tell me, but now that he had seen for himself what I was doing—that I wasn't being bribed and I was of no danger to the south—he felt that he could tell me.

I thought it was ridiculous. I had invited him to come to my meeting with Angela Teny. That must have persuaded him of my innocence. My first instinct was to laugh.

'You guys can continue to do your investigation and I'm happy to disclose everyone I've met and tell you who else I'm going to meet,' I said.

It wasn't until I returned to my hotel and went over the events of the day in my head that the anger hit me. I wondered if it had been my mistake. Maybe I hadn't sufficiently explained my intentions to people. I convinced myself that it wasn't their fault. I was keen to go to Juba now. I seemed to be on a blacklist of people to be watched, and I wanted to clear my name.

Riek Machar sent someone to pick me up from the airport in Juba. As we drove to his office, I stared out the window at the city with poor infrastructure, and buildings still scarred by wartime bullets.

I chose not to tell Riek Machar what my friend had told me. I didn't know if he knew. I had no idea who was responsible for sending the men to watch me, and I didn't want to betray my friend's trust. Instead, I repeated the same passionate words that I had uttered so frequently since I had arrived in Sudan. He responded positively, and the meeting lasted an hour or so. Then I was driven to my hotel.

Much of the hotel accommodation in Juba was actually tents. I was shown to the tent that was my room. After three years in Australia, I had almost forgotten the stifling African heat. I couldn't sleep. I dragged my mattress out of the tent and attempted to fall asleep beneath the sky.

■

I flew back to Khartoum the next day. The journey from Khartoum to Wau was not straightforward—and nor were the emotions I was feeling at the thought of seeing my parents again.

There was a small plane that flew to Wau. I had gone to the booking office and told them I wanted to leave in a couple of days. They said, 'You don't tell us when you want to go. We will tell you when the plane is ready to go.' They wouldn't leave until they had the numbers. They told me to keep my phone on and have my bag packed and ready to go at any time. I thought it was a crazy system, but I put my name down, paid for my flight and waited.

I got the phone call in the afternoon of my third day of waiting, giving me a departure time of 3 a.m.

What?? This airline is truly crazy, I thought. Why would a plane take off at 3 a.m.? But if I wanted to see my parents in Wau, this was the only way.

I wasn't taking any chances of missing my flight. I organised a taxi for 2 a.m. We were at the airport by 2.15 a.m. There were a few people at the airport but the check-in desk was closed. I thought that was very strange for a flight that was due to leave in 45 minutes.

I worried that I must be in the wrong place. I asked around, but the security guys assured me I was in the right place. So I sat and waited all morning, not daring to let myself fall asleep even though I was so tired. I kept going to the bathroom and splashing my face with cold water to force myself to stay awake.

The check-in desk finally opened at 7 a.m. The plane wouldn't take off until 9 a.m.—six hours after I was told that it would. I was fuming. But then I thought that soon I would see Mama, and this day would end happily, and I let the anger go. Baba would be there, too. He had come from Turalei to Wau especially to see me.

I went to the desk and politely asked the man in my broken Arabic: 'Why would you tell me to come at 3 a.m. when we're leaving at 9 a.m.?'

He looked at my travel documents and said apologetically: 'I wish we knew Australia is where you come from. We run into trouble all the time. The Africans never come on time, so we have to tell them to come hours earlier. But if we knew where you were from, we would have told you to come later.'

I could see his point. It made sense coming from a culture where time does not rule the people; the people rule time. In Africa, if you organise to meet at a certain time, people will turn up two hours later. It doesn't matter if you are on time; what matters is that at the end of the day we have met.

The man at the desk apologised and said he would ensure I was given the correct time for the flight back to Khartoum. I boarded the plane and forgot about my tiredness as the excitement of seeing my parents again took over. The plane was ancient, and I wondered if we'd get there at all. Some of the seatbelts were broken and I noticed there was a crack on the window beside me. I wondered, what kind of country permits a plane to fly in such a state?

Then I laughed at how Australian I had become and resolved to do what the Sudanese do: sit and chill.

The world's gaze remained locked on the violence that showed no signs of abating in Darfur. The United Nations identified about 130 000 newly displaced people just in the first months of the year 2007. It also reported hijacking of vehicles and attacks on humanitarian workers.

Medécins Sans Frontières was forced to evacuate a team of sixteen aid workers from the particularly troublesome town of Muhajariya in south Darfur after the town was bombarded in late 2007. More than forty patients in the town's only hospital had no choice but to flee. The attack also left more than 35 000 people in need of humanitarian aid, according to the organisation.

By the end of the year, a joint 20 000-strong peacekeeping mission by the United Nations and Africa Union was established in Darfur. But the violence continued.

18

Biological Strangers

The airstrip in Wau is sheathed in soil that is red and beautiful and steaming hot. When I saw the big, lush mango trees, I felt that I was finally home.

I had spent the hour or so on the plane trying to suppress my emotions—some of which I couldn't even identify. I wouldn't get to see Abuk, because it was a two-week walk to the village where she lived. Distressingly, I still hadn't even talked to her on the phone.

I wondered what my parents looked like and whether we'd know each other. As I stepped off the plane, I saw a man in the distance waving at me. It was Baba. I didn't recognise him until I was close enough to see his face. I had been a teenager when I last saw my father. He was with a boy I didn't know. I noticed that he had lost even more weight. In my heart, I felt happiness that he was alive. He smiled and walked towards me and extended his hand. I shook it as he said in English: 'How was your flight?'

I responded in Dinka and he was pleased. When we had left Wau, I hadn't been able to speak a word of his language. Now my Dinka was perfect.

'Where's Mama?' I asked.

'She couldn't believe you were coming,' he said. 'She refused to come because she said: "My Nyuol is long dead. I don't think he survived the war. Until I see him, I won't believe it. I don't want to go to the airport for a mistaken identity."'

The little boy had brought a bicycle. He put my luggage on the little carriage he had tied to the bike and we began the short walk to Mama's house. I looked around, searching for something familiar, something that would remind me that I was in my hometown. But I couldn't get my bearings. Mama had moved into another hut since the old hut had burnt down.

The only reminder that I was back home were the mango trees that I had climbed as a child—before the war had put an abrupt end to play. I saw houses that had been decimated into piles of burnt bits on the ground. I tried to control the emotions overwhelming me. I didn't want Baba to see my sadness.

People I didn't know stared at me as we walked past. I was shocked when strangers ran to me, weeping and speaking ardently in Bai. I didn't know what they were saying, so I stayed silent. They had been told about me, the son that Mama had given up for dead. Now he was coming home, and they wanted to see this miracle for themselves. The frequent interruptions lengthened our journey. We were walking with a posse of people rejoicing in my arrival.

The next thing I knew a strange woman in the distance was running barefoot towards me, sobbing loudly. 'That's your mother,' Baba said.

So I took off towards her. Like a scene from a cheesy movie, we ran to each other. I couldn't wait to hold her. And then she fainted.

I continued to run to her where she was now sprawled on her back. Someone poured cold water on her face and a few minutes later she opened her eyes. I looked into the face of the mother I hadn't seen for more than twenty years, hoping to see my own face. I searched for some resemblance, but couldn't see any.

She held out her arms and resumed sobbing and I fell into her embrace. She stared at me, a healthy-looking man. And then she spoke, and my father translated.

'Nyuol, come and sit on my lap,' she said, as though I were still the eight-year-old boy who had left her in Wau.

I looked uncertainly at my father, who gestured to me to do as she asked. So I sat on Mama's lap. It was quite awkward, a twenty-nine-year-old man sitting on his mother's lap while she reclined on the ground. I put my arm around her while she cried and touched my face over and over, still not believing it was me.

■

My grandmother was an elder in the compound and wanted to do a ritual, kind of like a ceremony, to welcome me home. There was chanting and praying, and then a chicken was slaughtered, cooked and eaten.

I was exhausted from being up all night at the airport. But still I didn't want to spoil their moment. So I let them dance around me, and then we had tea at the house.

I sadly observed that nothing had changed. My family were as poverty-stricken now as they had been twenty years ago. I don't know exactly how many of them were living together in this small, over-crowded hut, with barely enough food to survive, but there must have been about twenty people. They slept side by side on rugs on the floor. There was no electricity, and they bathed in the same way that I had detested as a child.

I couldn't keep my emotions in check. I excused myself and went outside to the toilet, which was really a hole in the ground near some trees. I stayed there for a few minutes, letting out the tears that I had held back. I didn't want my family to see me crying for them and their destitute lives.

I returned to the hut and gave them the presents I had bought in Khartoum—dresses for Mama, a radio and watch for Baba, and toys and clothes for my siblings. I gave each of my parents some money. And I gave the children lollies and balloons and tried to teach them the ABC song.

Mama cooked sorghum for me. It was a simple meal, but to me it was special because my mother had prepared it. It was made with love.

My family treated me like I was a foreigner, looking for clean water because they feared the water that I had routinely had as a child would now make me sick. But I had been drinking Western water for only three years; I thought my immune system could trump the African water. Still, I had taken malaria tablets and vaccines—medicine that my family had always lived without.

Mama asked me how I had survived. I couldn't bear to tell her. I felt I had to protect her from the truth. Knowing what had happened to me would have broken her heart.

I tried hard to speak in my broken Arabic, frustrated that I couldn't communicate with my own mother without Baba acting as an interpreter. I tried to ignore the signs of poverty everywhere I looked. I concentrated on the joy and resilience and pride I felt in the room. My family weren't going to let being poor break their spirits.

The following day they wanted to do another ritual, at midnight. This one was more serious and involved slaughtering a goat and smearing its blood on my body. My grandmother presided over the ceremony, reconnecting with the spirit that had helped me to survive the war. According to their superstition, we had to thank the spirit. Otherwise, I would die.

I was sceptical, but I went along with it again. I would have done anything to make them happy. They assured me that I wouldn't be harmed during the ritual, although there might be certain aspects that I didn't like very much—like having goat's blood smeared on my body. It would have been disrespectful to wrinkle my nose, so I endured the blood smearing.

There would be more chanting and prayers. 'For how long do we have to do this?' I asked. They told me we had to wait for a particular bird to come out. The bird would sing and perch on a tree, and then we would know our prayers had been accepted and nothing bad would happen to me.

So that night, I took off my clothes, my necklace, my watch and shoes. I walked in my underwear into the bush and they began chanting near a big tree. We were there for probably an hour before a bird actually did come from out of nowhere and—just as they said it would—perched on the tree and began chirping loudly. Satisfied that I was now protected, we went back to the hut.

■

My time with my parents was brief—just a few days. On the morning I was due to fly back to Khartoum and then Australia, I told Mama I'd come and see her again. 'I won't promise your suffering will go away,' I told her. 'I'm still a student and a refugee and I'm poor. But whatever I have, I will make sure your life is different from now on. Thank God you're alive.'

Mama came to the airstrip to see me off. My parents didn't ask me to stay in Sudan. They knew I had moved to a better life, and they were happy for me. Nor did they want to come to Australia. They didn't want to leave their Sudan.

Baba and I shook hands. Mama kissed me on the cheek and tearfully hugged me. I still couldn't bring myself to cry in the presence of my parents. I preferred to do my crying alone.

I flew back to Khartoum, my sadness interspersed with anger. I despaired over the lack of a future for the children in this country. The hatred threatened to flare again the closer we got to Khartoum—the city full of people that I felt were responsible for all of this. I fiercely fought the hatred. I knew if I let the hatred win, it would derail me and I would lose sight of the bigger picture that I had been working so hard for.

I thought that God had seen my pain and had rewarded me by letting me go to Australia. Being in a rich country had placed me in a better position to help my parents. God had done his part by keeping my parents alive. Now, it was my turn.

I carried the sadness for the entire journey back to Melbourne. I couldn't shake off the anger. I was angry with everyone but no-one. I didn't know where to direct my anger—at my leaders, or those we had been at war with. I was angry that war had permitted parents to be separated from their children. Seeing my parents had brought home just how much I had missed out on.

This was taken during the Western Tigers' inauguration, organised by Brimbank City Council. I am in the front row, second from the right.

Celebrating after scoring.

With the kids at the Breakfast Club. (Photo courtesy of the Brotherhood of St Laurence)

Telling my story as part of my work with the Brotherhood of St Laurence. (Photo courtesy of the Brotherhood of St Laurence)

The very emotional reunion with my mother in South Sudan. It was the first time I had seen her in more than 20 years. She still lives in a crowded hut in Wau, and I felt really bad when I saw her living in such a state. I'd love to build her a nice house one day, and I am now working on that. I want to surprise her. I hope I can do this before it is too late.

This photo with my father and my childhood friend Agel was taken in Turalei. Agel was living in Adelaide but has decided to move back to South Sudan.

With my partner Rose and our daughter, who was eight months old here.

With my great friend Emmanuel Jal, when he came to visit Melbourne in 2011 for a special event organised by the Brotherhood of St Laurence. (Photo courtesy of the Brotherhood of St Laurence)

I had missed out on being loved. Seeing my mother again had confirmed that I had little emotional attachment to her. I was trying to reconstruct the love that should have already existed. But I didn't know how to go about it.

I felt that I must be heartless because I couldn't love my own mother. I could easily relate to violence, but love was something I knew little about. I'm still trying hard, and I find peace when I share my story.

There are so many of us—parents and children who are strangers to each other. I keep in touch with my parents out of a sense of responsibility. Our conversations always have a practical purpose. We are strangers with a biological attachment. This is the price you pay when your family is ripped apart by war.

■

When I returned to Australia, life took on a different kind of toughness. I had a new resolve—and that was to do all I could to help my parents. I decided to defer university for longer and concentrate on working full time to help my family. I continued working at the furniture factory, sending money back to Sudan, while immersing myself in my Sudanese community work. Everything else in life stopped.

I moved back to the housing commission flat. I wanted to be close to my cousins as my work with the Sudanese community became all-consuming. There were two things driving me now: my impoverished family, and the dire conditions in which people in Southern Sudan were living. Questions about what I would do about my education—and my life—were on the backburner.

I felt the heavy weight of responsibility. Now that I had been reunited with my family, I was quickly confronting the full gamut of their woes. It seemed that there was always a new problem—someone was sick and needed money for medical treatment, or another relative needed money for food. Then the phone calls started coming late at night, from relatives or friends asking for help.

I had also developed a reputation as a Sudanese community leader in Melbourne. I had matured into a role model. People came to me if they had problems or needed someone to help defuse a situation.

I toyed with the idea of returning to Sudan to live. But now that I had deferred university, I thought there was little point. I'd be more useful to my country if I returned as an educated man.

My life took on a frenetic pace of working hard and continuing my community work. Tribal politics really kills me, and I became fixated on teaching people not to see other tribes as the enemy.

At the end of the week, I buried myself in soccer. My team still wasn't part of a competition, because we didn't have money and a home ground. So we played for the love of the game. It was my relief, my rare moment of fun. But I still longed to be part of a real competition.

I had never felt so driven, and I didn't have a spare moment to myself. But I preferred it that way.

At least the accusations of bribery had settled down now, as there was a deeper understanding in the community of what I was trying to do. Instead, there would be even more troubling issues to deal with.

While violent clashes continued in their country, the Sudanese would face a different kind of conflict in Australia. Still traumatised by their experiences with war, those settling in Australia had to contend with stories emerging in the media of Sudanese 'gangs' terrorising people, and Sudanese youths binge-drinking and engaging in crime.

In the months before the 2007 election, the Australian government said it would reduce Africa's allocation to thirty per cent of the total 13 000 refugees accepted in the entire program. Then–Immigration Minister Kevin Andrews controversially suggested that some African groups weren't 'adjusting into the Australian way of life'. His comments triggered fierce debate. Then–Chief Commissioner of Victoria Police Christine Nixon responded by saying that the Sudanese represented only about one per cent of people the police dealt with.

19

Ganging Up on Us

I will always remember 2007 as the year I discovered that my parents and Emmanuel were alive. It's also the year that I first saw Australia's true colours when it comes to race.

It came to a head when a Sudanese teenager named Liep Gony was bashed to death in the Melbourne suburb of Noble Park in September.

All year, stories had intermittently appeared in the media about Sudanese so-called gangs being violent and anti-social and causing trouble.

It is true that some Sudanese kids get intoxicated with alcohol, get into fights and can be disengaged. But this can be said about youth of all ethnic backgrounds. Drunk people are silly, whether they are drunk black people or drunk white people.

When I heard in the media about Sudanese gangs, I thought it was ridiculous. But I wanted to know for sure, so I began to do my own investigating. I wanted to know who was in these gangs. In response to my inquiries, the more common explanation was that they were just kids hanging out in groups. When people saw them together, they made the assumption that they were a gang. I could be hanging out with my soccer boys in a peaceful gathering, but someone would see twenty black men together and conclude that we're a gang.

When Liep died, there were some initial reports that he had been part of a gang and had been killed by a rival gang. Then it emerged that it was white hands that killed him.

I knew Liep. He was involved in some of the community activities I organised. He was a lovely boy, not a troublemaker, and loved playing basketball and hanging out with his friends. Some of his friends brought a basketball to his funeral. That scene pained me so much; it reinforced the senselessness of a teenage boy's life lost. A boy who had escaped the horrors of war-ravaged Sudan and come to a country that was meant to value freedom and security—only to die a brutal death.

I would have preferred that he had died from a disease or had been hit by a car, or had been recruited as a child soldier and died on the front line. At least then, his death would have had some meaning.

I had buried my own friends over the years without shedding a tear. But that day, at his funeral, I cried for Liep. And for the first time since I had arrived in Australia, I wished that I was back in Kakuma. I felt that I hated Australia the way I had been taught to hate the northern Sudanese.

At least in Africa I had been prepared for danger. My defences had been steadfastly up. Since moving to Australia, I had learnt that it was OK to put your guard down. Now, my brain was back on full alert, prepared for the enemy to strike once more.

I thought I had seen everything in Africa. I thought I was now incapable of being shocked by anything. But Liep's death shocked me. Violent death was normal in Africa. I struggled to comprehend how this could happen in Australia.

I became very cautious. I wouldn't go out very late. At least, not alone.

■

Some of Liep's friends howled for revenge. I prayed they wouldn't take matters into their own hands. His grief-stricken family handled the situation with dignity. Community elders cautioned against revenge, and used Liep's death as an example of what could go terribly wrong if you weren't careful. And then a politician set the issue alight all over again.

Liep had been dead for only a week when Kevin Andrews, then the immigration minister in the Howard government, ensured that the Sudanese community would remain on the front page of the newspapers. Andrews linked the federal government's recent cuts to the African refugee intake to the suggestion that people from countries like Sudan weren't settling and adjusting to the Australian way of life.

I read his comments in a newspaper, my anger growing. Why would a political leader say such a thing at a time like that? And then, as welfare groups and others loudly condemned his comments as a political stunt ahead of the 2007 election, I understood.

Sections of the media didn't help. That same week, the commercial television stations ran stories featuring video footage that they claimed showed a Sudanese gang violently taking over a liquor shop and stealing alcohol. Apparently, they were Sudanese men terrorising the workers at the shop. But the ABC program *Media Watch* picked up the issue and exposed the fact that the perpetrators weren't Sudanese at all.

It was beginning to feel like we were being targeted. After that, there was an incident where we were sitting in a car waiting for the traffic light to go from red to green. Someone in the car beside us observed our black faces, rolled down their window and yelled out, 'Hey, go back to your country!'

I had never felt that race was much of an issue in Australia. I wondered whether it was linked to Andrews' comments and the negative depictions of us in the media. If politicians could publicly say that we didn't fit in, did that give others permission to make us feel like we didn't belong here?

Up until now, I had experienced only a couple of race-related skirmishes. The first was soon after I got my driver's licence. I had borrowed my cousin's car and pulled into a petrol station one evening. I was about to pick up the pump when I heard a voice over the loudspeaker say that I had to pay first. No problem, I thought. I went inside and handed over my cash.

While I was pumping petrol into the car, two more cars arrived and immediately picked up the petrol pump as I had. I waited for the same voice on the loudspeaker. But it didn't come.

I was fuming, and determined not to let the man at the service station get away with it. I went back inside and said politely, 'My friend, what's the difference between me and them? Why did you allow them to pump first and not me? Is there a criteria you use to decide who has to pre-pay?'

While we were speaking, the other two customers had come inside, and were listening to our conversation. 'You made me feel bad,' I continued. 'Don't judge me and think I might not pay. Is it because of my race?'

The man behind the counter denied it was, and said the other two were regular customers. But I didn't believe him.

The man standing behind me was really nice, and told the man behind the counter: 'If you ask him to pre-pay, you should ask all of us.'

I turned around and thanked him. I was so angry that I sped out of the petrol station.

The second incident was on a train. I was reading a book and there were lots of empty seats around me. A large group of high school kids got on the train and took up those seats. They were talking and laughing loudly, but I kept reading.

One of the students moved to sit beside me. He took out his phone and held it in front of my book so I was forced to stop reading and look at it. There was a map of Australia with the words, 'Fuck off, we're full'.

'So what?' I said, maintaining my composure even though I felt like hitting him. The kids laughed and I snatched the phone, but resisted the urge to smash it. I wanted to act violently, but I knew it would undermine all my work in the community. So I gave the guy back his phone. Punching him wouldn't have been a good look when I had been preaching that violence wasn't the answer.

I stood up and moved away from them and stood in the middle of the train, thoughts flying through my head. Maybe they were right.

This wasn't my country, because I was just a refugee. I felt that I would never be at home in Australia.

I put these episodes together now and began to wonder whether Australia was a racist country. Some people in the Sudanese community say that there are Australians who are racist in a smart way. They're good at pretending that they're tolerant, while their racism is played out in less overt ways.

I concluded that most of Australia is overwhelmingly not racist, but there are certainly elements of racism in the community. And it's enough to make you feel sometimes like this isn't your home. Maybe these people are driven by an irrational fear of something different. Maybe they think we're coming here and taking what had been theirs, taking away their job opportunities.

It's a similar situation to when we had first moved to Pinyudo and Kakuma and the locals had hated us. At least in Africa, there was logic to their hatred—we were sharing their scarce resources. But here in Australia, there are plenty of resources.

I began reading more about Aboriginal people and what they had gone through. I thought that these were the people I should respect in Australia more than anyone. I remembered the first Aboriginal man I had met when I had just arrived in Australia, and how he had welcomed me. And I feel that the only people who have the right to stand up and tell me to go back to my country are Australia's indigenous people. I have a great respect for them. Whenever I see them around Smith Street near my work, I make a point of waving and saying hello. It's my way of saying, 'Thank you for letting me into your country.'

■

I didn't want to let Kevin Andrews off the hook. I tried to think of a way to get back at him. One day, I got my chance.

I was on a train on my way to Oakleigh, where I was doing some community work, when a friend called. 'Guess what?' he said. 'Kevin Andrews is going to be at a conference this morning in the city. A few of us are going to turn up and surprise him!'

I was in. I got off the train at the next station and headed back into the city. I wanted to do something that would grab attention and a headline. There was a small gathering of mostly white people outside the building, waiting for the immigration minister to arrive. They were holding posters and chanting, 'Refugees are welcome in this country!'

It was rush hour, and we were collecting a crowd of commuters who had stopped to hear us out on their way to work. I needed to Australianise myself to most convincingly make my point. I told my friend I needed Vegemite and white zinc.

'You're crazy!' My friend laughed, then went to a shop and made the purchases. I slapped the white zinc all over my face and quickly made myself a vegemite sandwich. A few minutes later, the minister arrived.

I recognised his face from the television. We moved towards him, chanting and blocking his way. I stood right in front of him with my white face and said: 'Is this what you mean by integration? Do you want me to be white?' And I held the sandwich to his face.

He didn't say anything. He looked a bit shocked. I must have been a very strange vision, a black man with a white face. But my actions were a crowd-pleaser. Passers-by approached me declaring: 'Good on you mate! This is your country, too!'

I got my headline. I was happy about that. The next day, my white face appeared, grinning, in the newspapers.

I received many congratulatory phone calls from community elders. But I was especially pleased that city workers had stopped and listened to what we had to say. I cared more about what my neighbours thought than the politicians. I was concerned that the government was driving fear into people. I wanted to get out the message that it wasn't true that the Sudanese were all violent and couldn't integrate. I told other Sudanese people to spread the word. 'Be brave and knock on your neighbour's door, have a cup of tea and tell them your story,' I said.

I thought it was the only way to end the fear.

Kevin Andrews' words made me all the more determined to make Australia my country. And there was no better way of doing that than by becoming a citizen.

I had long considered myself a stateless man. But Australia had opened its doors to me. Having citizenship would give me true freedom and a passport to travel anywhere. I remembered my desperate struggle to get out of Kakuma. I still can't believe that I can now pick up my Australian passport and go anywhere I like.

Being sworn in was an affirmation of my freedom; it confirmed that I would be a free man forever. My thinking changed too, as it made me feel that my place in Australia was not just temporary.

But still, they call me a refugee. Becoming an Australian citizen hasn't put an end to the label. I will always be a refugee, and I will die one. I thought the term 'refugee' had to have its end, because the word represents someone who is stateless and fleeing violence—whereas I am at peace and in my country. Still, the tag persists, and I have grown to accept it.

■

If something was driving me before, I felt it even more intensely after Liep's death. The news had even travelled back to Southern Sudan, of young people coming to Australia and wasting opportunities by forming gangs and getting drunk.

I spent a lot of time over the next year talking to young Sudanese people. My aim was to change the perception that Sudanese youth were intoxicated and violent troublemakers who couldn't integrate. I told them that kind of behaviour could have consequences for our brothers and sisters, still suffering in refugee camps, who were trying to come to Australia.

I started doing some part-time work at the Centre for Multicultural Youth with a youth interfaith program. All the while I continued my work with the Sudanese community.

News of the work that I was doing was spreading. Even overseas, to Jamila.

Throwing myself into work had been my way of coping with losing her. But I still couldn't forget her. When she heard about the work I was doing, she emailed me. She said that she had always known the kind of person that I would be, and wished me all the best.

Since she had got married, I had sent her the occasional cautious email to make sure she was OK. Sometimes she'd call me. Then we wouldn't talk for a while. She had asked around and heard that I didn't have a girlfriend. I didn't want one. I wasn't ready to let her go. She told me that if we had been meant to be together, then we would be. She urged me to forget her and move on. I didn't respond to that email. It made me too sad.

I later heard that she'd had a baby. She didn't tell me herself. But still, I emailed her to congratulate her. I still blamed myself for losing her. I should have been bold enough to fight for her.

I let Jamila know that I would always be there for her if she ever needed anything. We kept in touch. She'd send me an email when she heard about the latest thing I was doing for Sudan. She'd tell her cousins to check up on me to make sure I was OK.

Sometimes she'd call me when she was feeling down, and I'd try to make her laugh until she forgot her sadness. Early one morning she called me and blurted: 'David, I've discovered that to be more close to God is healing. It helps you let things go. You haven't let me go in your heart, and maybe that's why I'm having a hard time. I want you to let me go in your heart and move on.'

I laughed at her and teased: 'Are you OK?' And then I told her gently: 'I've let you go. There's no problem.'

■

I had started a drama class in Melbourne's south-east. One day a friend, Temar, came to rehearsal with a pretty woman named Rose.

Temar introduced us. Rose came to our rehearsals a few times after that, and sometimes we'd talk during breaks. I thought that she wasn't very talkative, and I could tell that she was a really nice person.

As we slowly got to know one another, I began to really like her and I asked her out.

We dated for a while. She was a Nuer, but I didn't care about tribal politics. Her family had fled from Sudan and gone to Egypt, so she hadn't had the refugee experience that I had, and she had come to Australia quite young. I wanted her to understand my story. So a couple of times when I was invited to speak publicly at events, I brought her along.

I was involved in so much around the community that sometimes it was hard to find time for our relationship. I told her from the start what my life was like, so that she could decide if she wanted to be part of it.

We became very close, and I fell in love with her. One night, I invited her to dinner to meet my cousin Archangelo, who I was living with. But we had to hide our relationship from most people because I was a Dinka and she was a Nuer. Her family wouldn't have accepted me.

■

I had continued my volunteer work with the Brotherhood of St Laurence. So when a paid job came up to coordinate the breakfast club, I was a natural for it. The organisation that had helped me get my first job in Australia now wanted to give me a job.

I quit my job at the furniture factory and focused on my new role, working on the program with Kate. My job included overseeing the volunteers, making sure there was enough food and sporting equipment, and looking after the wellbeing of the children.

The longer I worked on the program, the more I learnt about the children. We discovered that some of them weren't eating lunch, or didn't have an appropriate lunch. Our program got some funding and we started providing lunch as well. But we did this differently; we bought all the ingredients and taught the parents and their children how to prepare simple, healthy sandwiches with cold meats and salads, along with a piece of fruit and a bottle of water. It was about more than feeding children; it was about educating their parents, too.

I invested so much time working with the families, and it was more than a job for me. I loved my work. My role evolved into that of a community liaison officer, working with refugees and speaking at schools. The Brotherhood of St Laurence sent me to seminars, which exposed me to other organisations that asked me to do work for them. I learnt so much and took my new management and organisational skills back to my work in the Sudanese community.

I continued doing some work for the Centre for Multicultural Youth, which later nominated me to become a youth ambassador with the Victorian Equal Opportunity and Human Rights Commission. I had the opportunity to meet the then-commissioner, Dr Helen Szoke (now federal Race Discrimination Commissioner). We became good friends.

The more time I spent with Helen Szoke, the more I came to respect her. She was more than a personal friend to me—she was a mentor. She invited me to a number of functions and exposed me to lots of people, and asked me to speak at events. She saw something in me, and I feel that she will always be there for me.

Part of my role as a youth ambassador was to promote the new Victorian human rights charter in the community, and to tell people there was a place they could go to that dealt with complaints of racial discrimination. While I enjoyed talking to people about it, at the same time I felt that Australia's human rights record was perfect compared to the random killings that went on in Africa.

But now, the stories were pouring out. I attended community meetings in which Sudanese women stood and spoke of their experiences until they cried. One very bright boy spoke passionately about wanting to attend medical school. He was doing all the right subjects and getting good marks, but his teacher told him it would be too hard with his background.

By far, however, most of the complaints were about police, particularly in Dandenong and Noble Park. Young people in their cars were being pulled over by the police, and they didn't understand why.

I realised that a lot of the trouble between the Sudanese and the police was simply due to a lack of understanding of each other.

For instance, some of the young people didn't know that they couldn't sit around in certain public places with their friends and drink alcohol. They didn't know that there were rules governing drinking in public spaces. So when police told them they couldn't, they felt they were being harassed.

Other complaints were about employment. People felt they weren't being shortlisted for job interviews—even if they had the right qualifications—because they didn't have Anglo-sounding names. 'I guess I'm lucky,' I joked. 'My first name is David and my last is Vincent. Anyone would think I'm a white dude. Maybe you should try that!'

Helen Szoke came to some of these meetings and the Victorian Equal Opportunity and Human Rights Commission got some funding to investigate these issues. The result was a report called *Rights of Passage: The experiences of Australian–Sudanese young people,* published at the end of 2008.

The report was scathing. Among its main findings was that Liep Gony's death and the 'critical and even hostile attention' to the Australian–African community that followed had led to young people from those communities feeling more fearful. And they were increasingly reporting verbal or physical racist attacks in the public spaces they used, such as public transport.

The report also cited concerns by young Sudanese people that police discriminated against them by moving them on in public spaces more than non-Sudanese people, or stopping and questioning or searching them more often, and using insulting, racially-based language. The report did, however, make the point that sometimes the negative experiences appeared to be the result of misunderstanding and miscommunication.

After the report came out, the response from the police was fantastic. Helen Szoke and I attended many meetings with senior members of the Dandenong police, and they were willing to listen and make an effort to improve their interactions with the Sudanese community. One of the positive things that came out of it was soccer matches between police and Sudanese youth, so that they could get to know one another.

I think that the root of the problem was that we didn't know each other. I had my own frustrations, too. One time when I was involved in organising an event for Sudanese youth, it seemed that police cars were turning up every few minutes. It felt like we were being over-policed.

Many of the complaints from young people were about being pulled over for random checks, with no good reason. There were allegations that police in some cases were acting inappropriately, and they probably were. But the problem was that some of the youths were losing their tempers quickly. When they were pulled over, they became angry and agitated and confrontational. They just assumed the police were racist, when there could have been a problem with their car they didn't know about. So when the police asked them for ID, instead of giving it to them they'd angrily say, 'Why am I being pulled over?'

The situation would deteriorate after that.

We tried to educate people. If you're pulled over by the police, don't get angry and demand to know why. If you remain calm, the police will probably greet you politely and explain why they pulled you over and the whole thing will be over quickly. It is more likely that they pulled you over because your brake lights aren't working—not because you're black. I told them that if they had real problems, that's what the Victorian Equal Opportunity and Human Rights Commission was there for.

The Dandenong police offered to let some of us go on patrol with them, to give us an idea of how they did their job. It was a great idea, and I took them up on it. We drove around, and they would say, 'It's your turn now to pick out someone's mistake.'

There were also police multicultural liaison officers, whose job it was to bridge the gap between the police and the Sudanese youths. I got to know some of them and they were lovely people. The more we got to know each other, the more relations improved.

I think the hysteria over the Sudanese has subsided a little and the situation has improved. Much of it is thanks to the Australian public, some of whom have told me they were appalled by the comments made by Kevin Andrews.

Part of the problem I think was a fear of the unknown. People now have a better understanding of the Sudanese. There are more positive stories in the media about our community, and that has helped. I know now that when I sit on a tram beside a white guy, he'll most likely be happy to chat to me. It's sad when you see people on transport absorbed in their iPods, because it means they can't talk to each other. I wish people would spend more time talking to the person sitting beside them.

I have embraced Australia as my country. I don't care what anyone says because I know in my heart that I am doing so much to contribute to this country. I have a thicker skin; if you try to taunt me with racist remarks, I'll laugh and walk away.

Back in Sudan, tension was flaring in one of the most disputed areas in the Comprehensive Peace Agreement—the oil-rich Abyei area. As the north and the south hotly debated whether Abyei should remain part of the north or become part of a new South Sudan, fighting erupted between the Sudan People's Liberation Army and government troops. President Omar al-Bashir and Southern Sudan leader Salva Kiir agreed to international arbitration to help resolve the dispute.

It was decided that the residents of Abyei would have a referendum to choose what they wanted. But there was no agreement on the terms of the referendum, and it has never taken place. The area remains disputed.

Meanwhile, in March 2009, the International Criminal Court in The Hague issued a warrant for the arrest of President al-Bashir, on charges of war crimes and crimes against humanity in Darfur. Despite visiting several countries and exposing himself to potential detainment, he was never arrested. He denied all the charges.

20

Two Tribes, One Love

Rose and I continued to conceal our relationship. One day, the matter was taken out of our hands. She called me and told me she was pregnant.

'Congratulations!' I said. 'I'll call you back in ten minutes.'

I think she was worried about my reaction. But I was genuinely excited, even though I knew the fact that we weren't married would make it hard to tell her family.

I phoned my father. 'I have good news and bad news,' I told him.

'Tell me the bad news first,' he said.

'The bad news is I've impregnated a lady,' I said.

'Congratulations!' he said. 'What's the good news?'

'The good news is that I'm going to be a father!'

He laughed. 'Whatever I can do to help, let me know,' he said.

I wanted to marry her. Like me, my father didn't care about the fact that she was a Nuer—even though my grandmother had been killed by a Nuer in tribal clashes in Southern Sudan. He told me that if I loved her, I should marry her. Even though men from our tribe can have multiple wives, my father has always advised me to have just one woman. He must have heard stories about what a player I was in Kakuma. 'If you want a happy life without any problems,' he says, 'just have one wife!'

The problem was that my family didn't have many cows for a

dowry. I had told my father about Jamila, and I think he had felt bad that he didn't have the wealth for the dowry that would have given me the chance to marry her. And Rose, just like Jamila, was worth a large dowry because she was educated and living in a Western country. My father also warned me that intertribal marriages were difficult. There was a particularly large rift between the Dinkas and Nuer. My father was a Dinka and my mother a Bai, but that division was nowhere near as great.

I called Rose back and we had lunch together. I told her that I would support her. I knew we couldn't hide our relationship any longer. I encouraged her to tell her family, knowing our tribal differences would be an issue.

Rose told her family. My father also called one of her brothers to apologise, and to assure him that I was ready to get married. In our culture, you have to apologise by bringing some cows. But in Australia, I had to give them some money. It was a formal way of saying sorry.

Rose moved in with me in the private rental house I shared with Archangelo, and we later moved into a place of our own before our baby was born.

It took a while for Rose's family to warm to me. But I think it helped when they became aware of the work I was doing in the community, trying to promote peace in Sudan. I still can't marry Rose because there are formal celebrations we have to do first, and they cost thousands of dollars. It is hard to save when I am sending money back to Sudan. My father has recently had surgery and I have paid for his medical treatment. But I think it will happen. The important thing is that Rose is happy and living with me.

■

Our baby girl was born in early 2009. Around that time, I returned to university. Getting an education remained very important to me, and I could manage my schedule so that I could continue working at the Brotherhood of St Laurence and still attend my classes.

I went without lunch most days, so that I could save money to continue to support my parents. I'd have a cup of tea in the morning, skip lunch and not eat until dinner. I didn't feel hungry most of the time anyway. I was so overworked that sometimes I'd forget to eat. I was, in a sense, reverting to the life I'd had in Africa, surviving on one meal a day. It was like I was sharing my family's poverty—except in my case, it was a deliberate choice.

I was feeling more settled at university. Maybe it was because I had so many other things to worry about, I didn't have the time to indulge any lingering anxieties about fitting in. What persisted in troubling me most, though, was my family. I kept hearing new stories of their suffering, and it pained me.

I struggled to find adequate time to study and, inevitably, it shifted down my lengthening list of priorities. Still, I felt an urgency to pass and to finish my degree. I still felt as though I was doing three times more work than everyone else and I stayed up half the night scrutinising books. It was the only time I could dedicate to study.

I graduated from university that year, with majors in politics and criminology. Graduating is a really big deal in the Sudanese community, usually celebrated with parties. I was proud that I had a degree, but I also felt that education was so accessible in Australia. Even though it had been a really hard slog to get through it, I didn't feel like celebrating. I went to my graduation ceremony alone, received my certificate and walked out without taking any photos. I didn't even take Rose with me. That's just how I roll. Then I went home, sat on the couch, watched some television and went to bed.

It might have meant more if my parents had been there. I phoned Baba the next day and told him I had graduated. He was so proud. He said it was a really big deal for our family. I told him we'd celebrate when I got my PhD.

Each week I worked flat out Monday to Friday, and always looked forward to soccer on Saturday. It was my only respite from the relentlessness of my life.

We'd play a match and tease each other and argue over the English

Premier League and have a laugh and the occasional barbecue. I don't think it occurred to us just how skilful we were.

I was still playing with the Western Tigers, and my dreams of registering my boys to play in a real competition persisted. But over the years we hadn't been able to solve the problem of not having our own pitch. In order to register to be part of a competition, we needed a club and a ground and money and uniforms.

Our team's manager, Michael, had already dedicated a lot of time sending applications to a couple of councils, asking for help. That year, we applied again. The response was the most positive yet. Brimbank City Council told us there was a pitch under construction and when it was completed, the council might be able to accommodate us. There was no guarantee, but for the first time we had hope.

One Saturday evening, we were confronted with another good reason to have our own pitch. While we were training on a ground that wasn't ours, a white man came across the pitch with some of his mates. As we played, the ball nearly hit him. It was an accident. He then stood drinking in the middle of the pitch with his friends while we tried to play.

I went up to him and said: 'Mate, can you see we're playing?'

'Why are you playing?' he said. 'Why don't you go back to where you came from?'

His words got my friends fired up. They wanted to fight. But I tried hard to defuse the situation. 'You've made your point,' I said. 'This is not our country. We accept that. But you can't tell us to leave.'

He left and I thought that was the end of it. But he later returned with his friends and a big black dog, which he held back on a chain. 'Boys, I can see a problem,' I said warily.

I spotted two elderly people across the road and ran to them. 'Please can you be our witness?' I asked, explaining the situation.

'Son, we will be your witness,' the woman said. 'We'll call the police if you want.'

'No, later,' I said. I went back to the boys and told them to take off their boots and get changed. We were done for the day, and getting out of there. I was struggling to keep my temper in check, and losing the battle. The couple kept their promise and kept a watchful eye over what was going on.

The guy was walking towards us now with his dog—a dog that looked like it had been trained to hate people. He was restraining it on its leash. Some of the boys were frightened of the dog and quickly lunged into their cars. But I wasn't going to take any crap from this guy.

I moved towards him and he unchained the dog. I punched the guy and he jumped back, and when the dog came at me I kicked it and it actually recoiled. Then its owner came towards me again; I leapt at him and he retreated and began running and I chased him and chased him until I didn't think he'd come back.

I got in the car, trying to calm myself. I told the boys that if the police came I would make a statement. The police were never involved, but I regretted the way I had dealt with the situation. I felt bad about getting into a fight.

We never played on that pitch again.

Omar al-Bashir was re-elected President of Sudan in April 2010, amid allegations that the poll was rigged. Soon after his re-election, the International Criminal Court issued a second arrest warrant for the president, on charges relating to genocide.

The ICC's second warrant of arrest, in July 2010, alleged there were 'reasonable grounds to believe that Omar al-Bashir acted with . . . specific intent to destroy in part the Fur, Masalit and Zaghawa ethnic groups [of Darfur]'. It alleged there were reasonable grounds to believe that he was 'criminally responsible as an indirect perpetrator, or as an indirect co-perpetrator' of genocide by killing, genocide by causing serious bodily or mental harm, and genocide by deliberately inflicting conditions of life calculated to bring about physical destruction.

It also alleged there were reasonable grounds to believe that, as part of the government of Sudan's 'unlawful attack', government forces subjected thousands of civilians belonging primarily to those three tribes to acts of rape and torture, and contaminated the wells and water pumps of the towns and villages primarily inhabited by members of those groups.

Omar al-Bashir denied the charges. He later visited Kenya, which chose not to arrest him.

21

Freedom

Since we had reconnected, Emmanuel and I had been frequently talking about the continuing conflict in our native country. 'David,' he said during one phone conversation, 'there are so many of us around the world doing something. We need to bring them all together.'

We knew that 2010 would be a big year—it was the year before the referendum in which the people of the south would decide if they wanted secession. But the world's gaze remained on Darfur. We needed to shift it back to Southern Sudan.

I told Emmanuel that he was our great strength, as he was a star. We should use his name. But we needed others. Valentino's name came up. He had left Kakuma before me and had ended up in America. He had gained a public profile since telling his story in a book called *What is the What?* by Dave Eggers. I hadn't read the book, but I had heard about it and the great work he was doing. He was very passionate about education and had started the Valentino Achak Deng Foundation, and had built a big school in Southern Sudan.

I had already reconnected with Valentino through Facebook. I contacted him and told him about what Emmanuel and I were doing. Valentino was keen. The three of us began Skyping frequently. Our goal was to bring Southern Sudan back into the media. We were concerned that the upcoming referendum on the secession of South Sudan would reignite the conflict. We thought it was a ticking time bomb.

Through Emmanuel, other big Sudanese names became involved: Ger Duany, an actor and model living in the US, and US-based Olympic athlete Lopez Lomong. I had never met them, but they had been Lost Boys like us, and had gone on to achieve great things.

Together we started the Sudanese Summit, a conference that aimed to bring together young people to share ideas about promoting peace. I felt privileged to be working with these guys. The five of us regularly Skyped and swapped ideas. They were great ideas, but we weren't doing anything with them. A woman named Samantha Wiratunga was employed to be our project coordinator, and thanks to her we became more organised. Samantha and I spent a lot of time talking to each other and became quite close.

We each pitched in US$200 to get the thing started. Then we got some funding from a US-based foundation called Humanity United to host our summit near the end of 2010—just a few weeks before the referendum.

I wanted the summit to be in Juba. But we all wanted Sudanese people from the north and the south to attend, and security in Juba would be an issue. We were concerned that it might deter people from the north from coming. So we settled on the neutral territory of Kenya's capital, Nairobi.

We spent months organising the conference from our different continents. All five of us would attend. I lobbied young Sudanese people in Australia, and about ten came to Nairobi for the summit. After Nairobi, I planned to go to Sudan. I had taken unpaid leave from the Brotherhood of St Laurence to spend six months in Sudan, to help with the preparations for the referendum and to spend more time with my family. Helen Szoke was kind enough to lend me a camera and a laptop to take with me.

As I flew to Nairobi, I felt excitement—not only about what we were doing for our country, but also about seeing my friends again. We had arranged to meet for lunch at a fancy hotel in Nairobi. I was quite nervous.

'David, just be yourself, man!' I told myself. I turned up to the nice hotel dressed down in shorts, T-shirt and thongs. I timed it so I was deliberately late; I wanted to be the last to arrive.

The security guards at the hotel took one look at me in my thongs. I could almost hear them thinking, 'You're dressed like that and you think you're getting in here?'

I told them that I was there for a meeting. 'Who are you?' they asked sceptically. I told them I was Sudanese. They asked for ID, so I took out my Australian passport. They softened immediately. 'Sorry, sir!' they remarked, letting me in.

I walked in, and the first person I saw was a dreadlocked Emmanuel. My own dreadlocks were long gone. We grinned and hugged. 'Man, you're so fat!' teased Emmanuel.

'Emmanuel, I still can't believe you can sing!' I shot back. I wouldn't believe it until I saw it for myself.

I hugged Valentino. 'Good to see you!' I said. We talked about Noriaki. He had been a good friend to both of us.

I was introduced to the others, and told them it was a privilege to be there with them. I was so happy that we were all here; even though we'd gone our own ways, we'd never forgotten our country. Our love for our country was the centre of everything.

That lunch was unreal to me; we had been skinny kids struggling for food, and now we had people serving us good food in a nice restaurant. I went quiet as I thought about how far we had all come. At the end of the meal, we argued over who would pay. Valentino won the fight and got the bill.

Summit day was amazing. About 200 people turned up, and I was happy with the numbers, given the cost of travelling to Nairobi. People from the north and the south attended, and I was moved by their shared passion for peace. Valentino gave a beautiful speech about the work he was doing, and I enjoyed the connection with the young people from the north. Our enemies had become our friends.

The media attention was huge, thanks to all the stars in our group. I left the media to them, as I felt that I had no status compared to the other guys. I was satisfied that we had achieved our aim of getting South Sudan back into the media.

And I finally got to see Emmanuel sing. His dreadlocks went flying as he sang his songs of peace, and the crowd went mad. Wow, he really can sing, I thought. And then he beckoned me to join him, and I shared a stage and danced with the friend who for years I had thought was dead. I couldn't sing, but at least I could dance.

■

Word of our summit got back to the government of Southern Sudan, and a government staffer was sent to attend. He must have been inspired by what he heard, because he told his bosses that this summit should be happening in Juba.

It was quite extraordinary, but the Southern Sudan government chartered a plane for us to meet them in Juba, and told us they'd take us back to Nairobi when we wanted to return. All five of us who had founded the summit were men. I thought that it would be nice to include our sisters, so we invited some others who had been at the summit to come with us. In the end, a group of more than ten of us flew to Juba. To me, it felt like the first time the government had indicated it wanted to listen to young people.

When the plane landed, there were beautiful children there to greet us at the airport with music and dancing and flowers. I had managed to get away with wearing my thongs and shorts all through the summit. But now, I had reluctantly dressed up in nice pants and a shirt. Most of the others were wearing suits, and the girls looked beautiful in their suits and dresses.

We were driven to the Ministry of Peace where we met some people in the government. They wanted us to hold another summit in Juba, and offered to give us whatever support we needed. The summit had to be before the referendum, to unite us in our goal of achieving a peaceful separation. We were concerned that the referendum brought the potential for war from the north, which wouldn't want the oil-rich south to retain most of the resources. And if the referendum failed to bring secession, that, too, could prompt people from the south to react violently. We agreed that we had to be careful about what we said publicly. Saying the wrong thing could cost the lives of innocent people.

We were later invited to have lunch at the home of Madam Rebecca Nyandeng, the wife of the late John Garang de Mabior. She spoke beautifully in support of what we were doing.

We needed people to stay in Juba to organise the summit, which would be held in just a few weeks. The others looked at me; I had planned to spend the next six months in Sudan anyway, so it made sense that I stayed.

A really smart and articulate young woman from Melbourne named Nyadol, who had attended the conference in Nairobi, also stayed in Juba to organise the next summit with me. But it wasn't going to be easy. The first problem we encountered was a major division between some of the young people of Southern Sudan. There were about twenty organisations that we wanted to be involved. But we quickly learnt that if we invited certain groups to the summit, others might not attend. It wasn't a tribal division, but the politics were delicate. The division was more to do with the elders that the young people were affiliated with. So approaching all these groups when they weren't on good terms with each other would be tricky.

While all the others had flown home, Valentino had stayed in Nairobi for a while. He had some good contacts with young people and government. I called him and asked if he had any ideas about how to approach the various groups. He flew back to Southern Sudan to help us approach people, and explain to them what the summit was about.

I had known some of the guys heading the groups back in the refugee camps, and they were now living in Southern Sudan and doing great work. They were highly intelligent young people and they agreed that this was something that would unite us. We had grown up accustomed to a culture of violence. The last thing any of us wanted was another war.

A larger organising committee was formed, including Nyadol, Valentino and me. The Southern Sudan government gave us a plane to fly into all ten states in the south, to choose young people to attend. Nyadol and I spent a lot of time trying to manage the politics between the groups. We persuaded them that whatever their differences, the bigger picture was more important.

We advertised the summit through the media and put up posters throughout Juba. We used a few slogans in our posters, and some of them were based on the theme that our strength was in unity. The word 'unity' was one that no-one spoke of leading up to the referendum. It was kind of like a dirty word, as people believed it meant the north and south of Sudan being united as one country. But the idea we were trying to promote was unity within the south, because we remained divided and tribal conflict persisted. Still, the posters would get us into trouble.

∎

I was startled by a phone call at 1 a.m. It was from a friend who worked in government security. His bosses were concerned about the use of the word 'unity' in our posters. They wanted to know whether we had a hidden agenda. Were we opposed to secession from Sudan?

I tried to explain what we meant. He understood, but said that he had orders from his superiors that any posters containing the word 'unity' had to be removed before dawn. You couldn't argue with these guys. I hung up the phone and called Nyadol. The two of us drove around Juba until 3.30 a.m., pulling down posters while half asleep.

Despite all these hitches, the conference was a success. The discussion was very intense, and was focused on the issues of corruption and poor governance. President Omar al-Bashir had set up a Unity Support Fund, and there were some concerns about the possibility of the north throwing money at the people of the south to persuade them to vote against secession.

But our greatest priority was getting people to vote in the referendum in large numbers. There were people who wanted to vote, but they were in remote areas that were inaccessible by car, and a long walk from the voting centres. We resolved to go to villages throughout Southern Sudan and lobby people to vote.

There were villages that were so remote that I walked with friends for a day or two to get to them. It brought back memories of the walk I had endured as a little boy. But this time, I could see the benefits of the walk. And I knew where I was going.

I had taken six months of unpaid leave to do this, and my savings were depleted. But the village elders were welcoming and often gave us food, and we could camp anywhere with the tents we carried.

I walked with friends I had known in Kakuma, who had since returned to Southern Sudan. Some of them carried guns, but I refused—even though my father worried about my safety. I never wanted to touch a gun again. It became an issue when we were near the disputed border areas. My friends worried that I would be a liability by not carrying a gun. How could they protect me if we met the enemy? But I told them that carrying a gun would defeat the purpose—I had come to Sudan to promote peace.

I felt like I was playing an important part in making history. It was an amazing feeling, to join other young people who were just as passionate as I was, doing all we could to ensure that South Sudan became its own nation. Our parents and grandparents had fought for it to happen for half a century—since the 1950s and the first civil war. It brought everyone together in the south; I think it even helped to defuse tribal conflict temporarily.

I went to my father's district of Warrap state to cast my vote. The night before that historic day, I stayed up worrying about whether we had done enough to persuade people to vote.

But I didn't have anything to worry about. By 5 a.m. there were already long lines at voting centres. People were camping out and the queues were so long, I couldn't see the end of them. For many people, it was the first time in their life they had been given the opportunity to vote.

Nyadol called me from Juba, and said the city was on fire; people were running around celebrating before the results were even known.

I happily watched people cast their vote. It was done in a very peaceful manner. Young people stepped back and gave way to the elders, so they didn't have to wait for hours in line. Women ticked the box on the paper, then walked away crying. It was as if that simple tick officially marked the end of their suffering.

Then I took a long walk on my own and felt a sense of peace. In my mind, the result of the vote was a foregone conclusion, and I began getting ahead of myself and worrying about what would happen once South Sudan became independent. Because secession wouldn't solve the incredible poverty I had seen while travelling through Southern Sudan.

The voting went on for a few days. I waited until the very end, when the crowds had died down, to cast my vote. It had all gone so smoothly. And the people of the south overwhelmingly voted for secession. A few months later, the Republic of South Sudan became the world's newest country.

■

I didn't get to see much of my family during those months in Southern Sudan, as I was travelling so much. I dropped in to see my father when I could spend a day or two with him. He had moved from Turalei to Kuajok, where he had got a job. It was also closer to my mother's home in Wau.

Knowing I was physically close to them felt good; it was comforting for all of us. But the emotional attachment still wasn't there. And the desperate conditions in which they lived—despite the money I was sending them—continued to depress me.

Perhaps the most special moment was when my sister Abuk came to visit. She had walked on her own for several days to be reunited with the brother she hadn't seen in more than twenty years. It was a lovely reunion and I embraced her warmly. But it was the same story—I felt no emotional attachment to the little girl who had taken on the role of my mother long before she had become a woman.

Her years living in Turalei with my father's relatives meant she spoke Dinka. We swapped stories in our father's tongue—the language neither of us could speak as children but now spoke fluently.

After Baba and I had left her in Turalei, she had had it really rough. The war became very intense, and she didn't know whether we were alive. She had heard so much bad news, and had assumed that we were dead.

She told me that she had blamed our father for taking me away. She had thought it would have been better had we stayed, as then we probably would have lived. She had been angry when we had left without saying goodbye. But later, her anger had subsided when she understood that our father had left her there for her own protection.

While Turalei had been under fire, they had moved from place to place, returning when they could. She had never had the opportunity to go to school, and she regretted it.

My sister had children, too. A few days later, her husband arrived. I didn't remember him from Ethiopia but he remembered me because of the way I had played soccer. He had a phone, so Abuk and I could keep in touch when I returned to Australia.

The whole family went back to Turalei for another special ritual, to mark the reunification of our family. A spiritual leader slaughtered three bulls and there was lots of dancing as all the villagers joined our celebration, to give thanks to our ancestors for keeping me alive. They saw my return as a blessing; to them, being from the West and educated was a sign of someone coming home to find solutions to their problems, like a lack of clean water, food insecurity and poor levels of education.

Once again I felt the pressure of responsibility. I wanted to help my people. Some of the Lost Boys were returning to South Sudan to live, like my friend Dominic. As kids, we had run together from the bombs falling from the sky. He has returned to South Sudan from America, as an educated man. In America, William Machok started the organisation The Lost Boys Rebuilding Southern Sudan, and is building a school in the village he comes from.

I felt the pull of staying, and at one point even decided that I would move back to South Sudan, where I could do some great work with my education and skills. I received lots of job offers while I was there, and had been involved in some great projects.

I had been paid to do some work in a conflict mitigation program funded by the US State Department, mapping out conflict issues in South Sudan to help inform our new nation's security policy. People from all ten states were selected to run workshops, and I and another friend were given the opportunity to be part of it. I was also involved in helping to create the South Sudan development plan.

My heart might have been in South Sudan, but it wasn't practical for me to live there while my family needed me. The salary in South Sudan was poor. I thought that I could help my family in South Sudan more effectively by staying in Australia. The pressure of trying to meet the needs of my family had become quite intense. And it wasn't just my immediate family. My father and I recently worked out that the money I was sending them was helping to support about fifty-seven people. I also had Rose and our daughter to think about.

I have a younger brother studying at a university in Nairobi. I'm helping to support him. I hope that by getting an education, he will get a good job, and help me to support our family. That would relieve the pressure on me.

I always joke with my friends that I will never be rich. I've never had a holiday in my life. I'm looking forward to the day when I can go somewhere and just sleep all day, wake up and go to the beach.

We're all in the same situation, sending money to our families in South Sudan. In a way, we are forgetting our own lives in Australia.

The question I ask is, how long can I do this? We need to find a way to help people in South Sudan to sustain themselves. Much of it comes down to good governance, and having a democratic government that shares resources equally.

On 9 July 2011, the Republic of South Sudan officially became a nation in its own right, after the January referendum in which the people of the south overwhelmingly voted for independence. Sudanese president Omar al-Bashir said he accepted the results and the will of the people of the south.

But border demarcation remains a problem, particularly around the oil-rich Abyei, South Kordofan and Blue Nile areas. The splitting of oil revenue also remains unresolved. South Sudan has most of the oil resources, but needs to use the north's infrastructure to export oil.

In Darfur, the situation remains tense, despite the signing of a number of peace agreements with different groups. The most recent was a peace agreement in 2011, also known as the Doha Agreement. But not all the groups in the region agree to it. Among its main contents is a provision enabling the president to appoint a vice president from Darfur, the establishment of a new Darfur Regional Authority and a National Human Rights Commission, and paving the way for the future of Darfur to be determined through a referendum. It also cites an urgent need for the reconstruction of the war-ravaged region and the return of its displaced people.

Meanwhile, in late 2011, Kenyan High Court judge Nicholas Ombija ruled that Sudanese president Omar al-Bashir should be arrested and handed over to the International Criminal Court if he ever set foot in Kenya again. President al-Bashir continued to deny the ICC's charges.

22

Dreams and Discipline

While I was in South Sudan, I got a phone call from one of the soccer boys, who had some exciting news: Brimbank City Council had found us a home ground. The council had approached the Sunshine Heights Cricket Club, which had a pitch. And they were happy for us to use it.

Chris Hatzoglou was the club's president and his brother Nick the vice president. They came from a family of Greek migrants, and had been moved by the story of the Sudanese soccer team that had spent almost seven years trying to find a home ground. They knew we had no money, but they wanted to give us a chance. Following their enormous act of goodwill we became the Sunshine Heights Western Tigers Soccer Club.

Now that we had a home ground, plus funding from the council and Football Federation Victoria to help us buy uniforms, we were eligible to join the Metropolitan League North-West competition.

I couldn't wait to get back to Melbourne. But the excitement was tainted with uncertainty—I didn't know how our team would go in a real competition with white boys and proper rules. As one of the most experienced and skilled players, I had by default become the coach. And I knew my boys had issues with discipline. There had been occasional misunderstandings in the team, but lack of discipline wouldn't be tolerated in a real competition, as we found out later.

By the time I returned from South Sudan in May 2011, the season had already started. I resumed my position as the coach, even though I'd missed a couple of months. Michael remained the manager.

I met up with Nick and thanked him, and told him how much it meant to all of us to be part of a real competition. The boys were doing very well and winning lots of games. We had registered almost thirty players, so we had enough for a seniors and a reserves team. I played occasionally, if some of our boys were injured.

We were top of the ladder all year, and I couldn't believe how well we played. We had vastly underestimated our ability. But my concerns about discipline were confirmed.

During one game, one of our boys was kicked and fell, and he later said that a guy from another team had said to him, 'Get up, you black cunt!' So he got up and went *BANG* and punched him. The next thing we knew, there was an all-out brawl between the two teams.

During another particularly rough game, one of our players entered a verbal slanging match with an opponent. We won the game, but our boy later told us that one of the guys in the other team had shouted after the game, 'Go back to your country!'

Our boy replied to the guy, who came from another ethnic team: 'You're not Australian!' And it was on. They began shoving each other and other players joined in and it descended into a melee.

Both incidents ended up at the tribunal and all the teams involved were punished. We copped big fines and lost points. And that's how we lost the season in the end: we won the final nine–nil, but finished second on the ladder on points.

Soccer is a game of tactics and other teams have worked out how to get to us while we are on a winning streak—by calling our boys names and making them lose their tempers. They use it as a weapon against us, to put us off our game. Our boys become angry young men and get distracted, and I have to find a way to bring them back into the game.

I attribute some of it to the violence they were exposed to as children. When you're raised in a war zone and trained to be a soldier, your instinct is to respond to a situation with violence. My boys knew nothing different. As the coach, my greatest challenge is to teach them to control their anger. It's a big task, but I know the boys respect me and I can work with them.

The Sunshine Heights club were concerned about discipline too. Michael and I told the club that we were working on it. I am trying to get the boys to think differently, to keep a cool head and learn to walk away. Whatever your opponent says, prove him wrong with your skills.

We developed a policy that when boys get into fights, they get suspended. I don't want them to play if they're going to be hot-headed. It is better for us to lose with dignity than to get embroiled in fights that leave us with big fines that we can't afford, placing more pressure on Sunshine Heights.

Still, I am proud of how our boys have played. It's a big deal for a team of refugees to come from nowhere, have a stellar season and be elevated to a higher competition in its first year. And I love that at the end of a game we can shake hands with the white boys and they can appreciate how skilful we are.

I feel that we will be better prepared in 2012, now that we've had a taste of playing in a competition with firm rules. We will have to play at a higher skill level and the stakes will be higher, too. We won't put up with the boys in the team indulging their tempers on the field.

I've told the boys that we either play in the competition just to participate, or we compete to win. If they want to win games, then they have to change their attitude.

Usually when a coach chooses his team, skill and fitness are the most important factors. But this year, the number one quality I looked for in selecting my senior team was discipline. The second was commitment to training and the third was skill. If our best players don't have any self-control on the field, they will not play. I want boys who can listen and demonstrate sportsmanship. I'm confident that I can work with the other boys to lift their skills. I know it's a huge risk to choose discipline over skill, but a lack of discipline will cost us.

Since I had this chat with the boys, I've noticed an improvement in their attitude. They began competing hard because they wanted to be selected in the team.

This is about more than soccer; we are trying to teach the boys about life skills, and the bigger picture. If they can learn to control their anger on the soccer field, then they can learn to respond appropriately to all situations in their lives.

I see soccer as a way of engaging these boys. When they play well, it's a self-esteem lifter and it gives them a sense of purpose. I'm looking for more ways to engage the boys, with regular outings to build team spirit. Some of the boys are really good; all they need is some exposure.

I have a bigger dream for the team. I'm working on trying to get them a game in South Sudan. I want to expose their talents there, in the hope that some of them could one day play for the South Sudan national team. I'd also like to try to forge relationships with some clubs in the Victorian Premier League, to see if I can get the boys to train with them.

I feel that I can live the dream that I once had through these boys. I want the Sudanese community to get behind us. We also need to establish a South Sudanese soccer league, because there are a number of teams here that aren't part of a proper league.

I've asked Lueth to be a mentor to the boys and he has agreed. He has always been someone I looked up to—ever since the days I played with my socker ball in Pinyudo, watching the big boys play, dreaming of playing with them.

■

I was honoured when the Victorian Equal Opportunity and Human Rights Commission nominated me for the People of Australia Ambassadors program, which aims to promote multiculturalism in Australia. In January 2012, Prime Minister Julia Gillard announced the forty Ambassadors. I was one of ten people chosen from Victoria.

I want to use this opportunity to advocate on behalf of refugees. I wish we could be humane and look at asylum seekers who arrive in Australia by boat as people who are desperate and need help. I'd like the Australian government to find a way to process them from their countries faster so they can come here safely, instead of risking their lives by attempting to come to this country by boat. But I also understand their desperation when they choose to make the journey by sea.

I feel that Australians are generous, and I'd like to thank the Australian people for opening their doors and welcoming us, and giving refugees a second chance at a good life.

My friend Noriaki continues to inspire me. Together with a friend from Japan, a woman named Aya, I'm working on plans to build a centre in South Sudan called the Noriaki Multi-Purpose Centre. It would mainly be used for sports, because that was Noriaki's passion. I'm discussing it with a number of people in Japan, including his parents. We spoke at a conference in Japan in May 2012 to help raise the funds to make the centre happen. I have started a charity called Peace Palette. It aims to promote peace in South Sudan and engage youth through sport, art and drama.

I remain hopeful that there will be reconciliation between Sudan and South Sudan, and I'm still talking to the South Sudan government about this. Both nations have much in common, and share a history and a border.

I'd like to spend more time working in conflict resolution. I recently left the Brotherhood of St Laurence to spend more time working with African communities in Australia, helping them to enjoy a proper settlement here and creating a vision for themselves, while keeping in mind where they came from. I've already been doing conflict resolution training with some African communities, in collaboration with the Neighbourhood Justice Centre.

I hope to take some of that work back to South Sudan, where tribal conflict persists. I am returning to South Sudan to run minisummits with young people in each of the ten states. The main theme will be how to stop young people from engaging in violence, particularly tribal conflict.

Much of it comes down to cattle. Cows are money in South Sudan. Quite often, a tribal feud will begin when one tribe steals another tribe's cattle. Then the fight intensifies and people are killed. I wish the tribal conflict would end. We don't need to reproduce the experiences of the past; we need a generation with a new understanding, like the Sudanese summit that my friends and I started. It is made up of different tribes—Valentino is a Dinka like me, and Emmanuel is Nuer.

Occasionally, I think about my friends and it pains me. I feel bad about what we all went through, but I don't blame anyone. I want to protect children, and do what I can to ensure that children are no longer trained to be soldiers anywhere in the world. But at the same time, I recognise that being trained as a soldier helped to make me strong. It helped me to survive the toughest ordeals.

My story is not the worst story. There are people out there who have had a tougher life than mine. I'd like people to think about what they can do to help change someone's life.

Even now, I continue to have unresolved trauma. Just the other day I was driving, and my father called me. A simple conversation with him was enough to bring back memories of my childhood and the separation from my parents.

I hope that people can learn from my story. And that knowledge gives me strength. I feel that I have come so far, and I want people to be challenged by my story. I want the younger generations to fight for causes they believe in.

Those memories are part of me, and they fuel my passion and push me to work harder. There may be unpleasant memories in your life, but I believe that you can turn them into positive energy.

■

Emmanuel remains one of my great friends. But my state of Warrap and his state of Unity in South Sudan are still at war with each other. A lot of it comes down to tribes fighting over cattle. We are trying to find solutions to end the tribal warfare, and we are organising a soccer match between our states on World Peace Day in September 2012.

It's a way of bringing our communities together. Emmanuel and I have agreed that towards the end of the game, we will each play for our states—just like we played together as little boys. But now, we'll be playing for peace.

Epilogue

I want my daughter to know my story, and I want to take her to Africa when she is old enough. I want her to grow up knowing where I come from. It will be very special taking her back to the camps in Ethiopia and Kenya and showing her where I grew up. I want her to see for herself what my life was like, and make her own decisions about the person she wants to become.

It was such a great joy to have her. I remain close to Father Patrick, and I asked him to baptise her. People say that she looks like me. The fact that I didn't have a good childhood makes it all the more important to me to ensure that she lives a very happy life and enjoys all the things that I didn't.

Her skin reflects the fact that she comes from a different race to many Australians, but I want her to grow up knowing she is Australian and can do anything she likes. I want her to know that she is lucky to have been born in Australia, but I also want her to know her roots, and just how difficult life can be.

I don't mind if my daughter chooses to bring home a white man. And if she decides to get married, there will be no dowry. But it would make me sad if she forgot her roots, grew up not respecting her elders or was consumed by the glamour of life in Australia. Education has always been very important to me, and as long as she is doing well at school she can be whoever she wants to be.

I also want my partner Rose to be the person she wants to be. The fact that we are from different tribes remains an issue. I think Rose gets it tough from people sometimes, and I feel protective of her. I wish people could see beyond tribal differences.

Rose and I speak to each other mainly in English—we can't speak each other's tribal languages. Our daughter spends a lot of time with Rose's family, so she will probably pick up Nuer before she learns Dinka. But I don't mind. She is repeating the pattern that I went through as a child. We learnt Mama's language because we were with her family and Baba wasn't around much. But now I speak my father's tongue fluently. Maybe she will eventually learn my language.

I have a strong emotional connection to my daughter—the type of connection I was deprived of. Every child has the right to live with their own family, and to be loved by their parents.

According to our culture, the father gets to choose his child's name, and consults his own father. Often a child is named after a respected older person. I wanted to give my daughter a traditional name, so that people would know where she came from.

To me, my sister Abuk was a hero. During the war, I had been with my father for at least some of the time. But Abuk had been forced to survive without either of our parents.

I named my baby girl Abuk.

Author's Note

Writing this story has been an emotional journey for me and to write it I needed to remember back to difficult times, to make connections with my past and to find out facts that I had never previously known. It was only in researching this book and talking to my father about my childhood that I learned I was born in 1978 where previously (and recorded on my passport and at the camps) I believed that I was born in 1983. Fortunately my father had kept a record of our births. In earlier interviews, before the writing of the book, I had always thought that I was three or four when I left the Sudan but I now know that I was eight.

Much of this story is based on my recollections as a child and, where possible, I have spoken to my father and friends around the world who were similarly resettled from the camps to verify events. The quotes throughout the book are a true translated reflection of the intent and tone of what was happening at the time and not verbatim, as it would be impossible for me to recollect one hundred per cent word-for-word conversations that took place many years ago often under very difficult circumstances. Some names have been changed to protect people's anonymity.

I wrote this book in the hope that readers would be able to understand not only how my life was but how the lives of many Sudanese children were.

Acknowledgements

I have come a long way to be where I am today. I would not have achieved all that I have without the support I continue to receive from so many people and organisations. I would like to thank the following: Archangelo Nyuol Madut, for sponsoring me to come to Australia; Rozalin Nyakulit Joshua; Father Patrick; Dr Visier Sanyu; Sara Maher; Dr Helen Szoke; Jackie Lane; Nick and Chris Hatzoglou; Rob and Cheryl Wood; Mike and Jean Brown; Nigel Heywood; Nyok and Kathryn Gor; Biong D Biong; Michael Apuot; Emmanuel Jal; Valentino Achak Deng; Samantha Wiratunga; John Mills; Lynley Brophy; Agel Ring Machar; William Deng; Nelson Kur; Awak Ring Mathok; Carolyn Pickett; Jo MacFarlane; Paul Daly; Aya Ono; Sharon Shaw; Kate Polack; Bernadette Nunn; Dr Susannah Tipping; Jay Jordens; Nyadol Nyuon; Carmel Shute; Faten Mohamed; Tania Miletic; Ida Kaplan; Scot Thornton; Heather Stock; Sarah Lewis; Tara Willersdorf; Samuel Lueth; Therese Hammond; Kate George; Father Jeff Ohare; Fetu Paulo; and Mary Lawry. Also, thanks to my father, Vincent Mangok Ayuel, for filling in some missing pieces.

I would also like to thank the Brotherhood of St Laurence, Fitzroy Learning Network, the Victorian Equal Opportunity and Human Rights Commission, Centre for Multicultural Youth, Initiatives of Change Australia, Neighbourhood Justice Centre, Sunshine Heights Cricket Club and the Western Tigers.

In researching this book, the following sources were useful in providing background on the political and humanitarian crisis in Sudan, and other information: *The Root Causes of Sudan's Civil Wars* by Douglas H.Johnson; the Office of the United Nations High Commissioner for Refugees; Médecins Sans Frontières; Human Rights Watch; the Inter-Parliamentary Union; Amnesty International; the United Nations;